The
Trees of
CHRISTMAS

The Trees of CHRISTMAS

Text Compiled By *EDNA METCALFE*

Photographs By Al Clayton

Howard Graff, William B. Witsell

Richard T. Lee

Abingdon ♪ **Nashville**

THE TREES OF CHRISTMAS

Library of Congress Cataloging in Publication Data

METCALFE, EDNA.
   The trees of Christmas.
   Bibliography: p.
Includes index.
   1.   Christmas trees.   I.   Title.
   GT4989.M47 1979 394.2′68282′O28   79-12288

ISBN 0-687-42591-3

Photographs of the United States Community Tree and the Lithuanian
Tree courtesy of *House Beautiful*

MANUFACTURED BY THE PARTHENON PRESS AT
NASHVILLE, TENNESSEE, UNITED STATES OF AMERICA

PREFACE

The Christmas tree is one of the world's most beautiful and expressive Christmas symbols. In it are captured the sacred and secular, the rich varieties of national and regional traditions and festivals, fact and folklore, the simple and the sophisticated.

Just as the observance of Christmas itself has evolved out of many influences through the centuries, so has the decoration of the Christmas tree taken many distinctive forms as people have supplemented the traditional with their own original touches. *The Trees of Christmas* brings together twenty-three traditional and contemporary interpretations of the Christmas tree, and represents a broad sampling of countries, regions, and themes.

Some of the countries included in this book are now behind the so-called "Iron Curtain," and in these Christmas may not be observed as widely as in former years. However, traditions are slow to change, and, as in America, are carried on by descendants of those who have emigrated to other countries.

Each tree is accompanied by descriptive text on the country, customs, or theme which inspired its decoration. In addition detailed instructions are included for construction of all handmade ornaments. The reader should note that most ornaments are designed for exhibition trees, which generally are larger than those used in the home. Where smaller trees are desired, the construction dimensions should be scaled down proportionately.

—The Publishers

ACKNOWLEDGMENTS

The publishers wish to acknowledge their indebtedness to:

The Horticultural Society of Davidson County, Tennessee, whose annual exhibit "Christmas Trees of Many Lands" was both the inspiration for and basis of this book;

"Cheekwood," the Tennessee Botanical Gardens and Fine Arts Center, in Nashville, Tennessee, the gracious setting in which "Christmas Trees of Many Lands" was exhibited and photographed.

CONTENTS

Deep in the winter night, the family will come one by one,
carrying great and small boxes, brilliant in all colors,
ribboned in red and green, silver and gold, bright blue,
placing them under me with the hands of their hearts, until
all around me they are piled high, climbing up into my
branches, spilling over onto the floor about me. In the
early morning, with all my candles burning and all my brilliant
colors standing out and twinkling in their light, the
children in their pajamas and woolen slippers rub their
sleeping eyes and stare at me in amazement. The mother
with her hair hanging down her back smiles and glances
here and there, and the father looks up and down at me,
quiet and pleased, . . . for I am the Christmas tree.

from *The Book of the Year*, by Fritz Peters

AUSTRIA

In Austria Christmas means a whole month of joy and excitement as well as religious feasts and fasts. Saint Nicholas, the good spirit and gift-giver for Austrian children, and his companion Krampus, who visits naughty children, arrive on December 5. This day marks the beginning of the Christmas season with the Festival of Saint Nicholas. On December 6 the markets are opened with a wonderful array of ingenious toys and foods, and the celebration continues until Epiphany, January 6, when the Wise Men appear. The *Christkind* brings gifts on Christmas, even helps to decorate the tree.

The country of Austria has been known through the years as a land that is full of folklore. People in the most remote farm and mountain regions are steeped in old practices which have come down through the centuries, and they play and sing the tunes which have been known from generation to generation. Around the Advent season this folklore is seen at its height as Austrians continue the practices of their ancestors. A ceremony is held to protect the countryside from the mischievous spirits which wander about on Christmas Eve. Half an hour before midnight fireworks are lighted, bonfires are kindled and guns and hand mortars are fired. Wicked spirits are smoked out of barns, and the initials of the Wise Men are written over the doors for further discouragement. Offerings of food and wine are made to fruit trees, and in some parts of the country food is put out for the four elements of air, fire, water, and earth.

The Advent wreath is the first outward sign of the season, and there is great festivity as the first candle is lighted on the first Sunday in Advent. The Nativity scene is found in every Austrian home during the season; very often the crèche has been in the same family for many generations, having been carved in wood centuries ago. New pieces are carved from time to time so that in some homes the crèche contains not only the Holy Family but any number of other figures. To the Austrian the Christ Child is theirs, born somewhere in their valleys at Christmas time long ago, and being born again each year. Their songs tell of the gladness of his birth.

It was during the Christmas season of 1818 in the village of Oberndorf that Franz Gruber gave to the world the music of the beautiful hymn "Silent Night." The story goes that the church organ was unfit for use and the priest, Joseph Mohr, talked over the situation with the young organist, Franz Gruber. As Mohr walked through the fields, wondering what to do for music for the Christmas service, the words of the lovely hymn came to him. The next morning he repeated the verses to Gruber, who immediately wrote the melody. That night, on Christmas Eve, Mohr sang his song to the accompaniment of Gruber's guitar.

The tree is the bright jewel of the home at this happy season. The popular custom is for the Christmas tree, which is usually fir or pine, to be kept in a locked room until Christmas Eve. The tree is decorated by the parents with gold and silver garlands and a large number of candles. After the Christmas Eve supper, the father reads the story of the *Christkind* to the family, guests, and servants. Then a bell is rung, and the tree is exhibited in a blaze of glory.

The presents are spread out beneath the tree. In wealthy homes each member of the household may be assigned a table holding wrapped gifts and every kind of sweet. It is the custom for the family, standing in front of the tree, to sing Christmas songs, usually "Silent Night," "O Tannenbaum," and many other peasant or classical carols.

High in the Austrian Alps at midnight on Christmas Eve the most distant mountaineer lights a torch and makes his careful way to the home of his nearest neighbor. There he is joined by the members of that household, also bearing lighted fagots, and they continue toward the village, adding to their number at every house along the way. From the valley the light is seen winding down the mountainside, and the melody is heard which proclaims that Christ is the messenger of peace. At the end of their journey the mountaineers join with the villagers and proceed to the church, where the Christmas service begins.

NATIVITY SCENE DECORATION

MATERIALS:

6″ styrofoam ball, cut in half
gold braid, trimmings, gold cord
gold paint
cut-out Nativity scene

DIRECTIONS:

1. Paint the outside of the ball gold.
2. Set a cut-out Nativity scene in the hollowed-out ball, placing it about a half inch inside so that surrounding frame gives it depth.
3. Trim the opening with gold braid. A 6″ ball may be trimmed with a 2″ band of lacy metallic ribbon plus a sequin-loop braid. Embellish the hanger with a spray of balsam or greenery of the tree.
4. These may be made in smaller sizes—3″ and 4″—for variety.

WINDOW BALLS

MATERIALS:

6″ styrofoam ball with windows
3″ plain styrofoam ball
velvet ribbon, ½″ wide
4 gold angels, 2″ high
gold spray
gold braid, rickrack, or circlette edging
4″ gold foil tassel
foil leaves
sequins

DIRECTIONS:

1. Spray the two balls with gold paint, add sparkle at random over the surface of both. Scatter glitter or sparkle inside the window openings.
2. Frame the openings in the large ball with gold metallic braid, rickrack, or circlette edging.
3. Run bands of velvet ribbon between the

windows from top center to bottom of ball. In the four sections thus marked off make decorations using foil leaves and sequins.

4. Glue an angel in each of the four openings.
5. Attach the small ball to bottom of the large one. Finish the bottom of the ornament with a gold foil tassel and finish the top with a bow of velvet ribbon and a wire for hanging.

KRIPPS

MATERIALS:

plastic fruits—apples, pears, oranges
small Nativity scene, angels, etc.
self-adhering velvet ribbon
gold or silver spray paint, gold cord, trimmings

DIRECTIONS:

1. With a razor blade cut an opening in side of fruit approximately 1½" wide and 1¾" high. There is a plastic fruit with a velour finish which makes a handsome ornament.
2. Spray inside of fruit with gold or silver paint and allow to dry.
3. Frame the opening with strips of velvet ribbon. Glue gold or silver trimming to the ribbon.
4. Cut a small-scale scene about 2" x 2½" from a Christmas card. Edge with narrow trimming such as soutache braid.
5. Fill back half of fruit with crumpled tissue paper, then carefully curve the small picture so it will go into the fruit.
6. Put together two pieces of green self-adhering velvet ribbon 5½" long and ¾" wide. Cut the ends in the shape of leaves, then tie the ribbon strip around the stem of the fruit. Add a gold cord for hanging.
7. Small angels may be hung inside the fruits against a background of angel hair. Run a small wire around the angel, then through the top of fruit to the stem.

DENMARK

The Christmas season is joyful and busy in Denmark. The people consider Christmas their greatest festival of the year and enjoy elaborate preparations for its observance. Christmas Eve is a time of chiming church bells, family dinner, the ceremony around the tree, and hymns and carols in candlelit churches.

There are no preliminary festivals such as the day of Saint Lucia in Sweden, but the main business streets are gay with holiday displays and the confectioners' shops are colorful with fruits and flowers of marzipan, the choicest of Denmark's Christmas sweets. The first harbinger of the season is the great Baking Day. Every Danish home becomes virtually a bakery about the middle of December, but Baking Day is something special. On that day the housewife mixes the dough for *Brunekage*, a paper-thin spice cookie served in all Danish homes at Christmas. The mixing is done two or three weeks before the baking so that the dough may ripen and the flavors meld. A recipe given by a Danish housewife will yield three or four hundred cookies, for in this hospitable country one must have a plentiful supply of food. As in Sweden, every visitor to the home must be fed lest he bear the Yule spirit from the house. This would be a tragedy because it could not be recaptured until the next year.

On Christmas Eve the family gathers for an early meal. The Danish flag decorates the home as well as the Christmas tree. The lighted candle in the window offers food and shelter to travelers who may be passing, in the spirit of the Christ Child. As the twilight falls, the father reads the Christmas Gospel, and in the darkening room the family sings the Christmas songs dear to their hearts, such as the one by their own poet Hans Brorson:

"Thy little ones, dear Lord, are we
And come thy holy bed to see.
Enlighten every soul and mind
That we the way to thee may find."

The first course of the dinner is the traditional rice pudding with a whole almond in it. The one who finds the almond keeps the others in suspense until all the porridge is eaten. Then he announces his prize triumphantly and claims the reward—usually a fruit of marzipan. The rest of the dinner consists of goose stuffed with apples and prunes and served with red cabbage, potatoes, and lingonberry sauce.

After dinner is over, the father and mother disappear into the locked parlor or living room. Then the doors are suddenly flung open and there is the gleaming Christmas tree. The youngest child is the first to enter the room, then all the family clasp hands and circle round the tree singing Danish songs and carols.

On Christmas Eve when the rice pudding is served, a bowl of pudding is ceremoniously set aside for the *Nisse*. Like the Swedish *Tomte*, the *Nisse* is a barn elf or sprite who keeps a friendly eye on the animals in the barn or other domestic animals in town or country. The *Nisse* bears some resemblance to Santa, with his red stocking cap and long white whiskers. He is pictured on Danish Christmas cards and decorates the tree.

In some parts of Denmark there is an interesting custom of "blowing in the Yule." At sunrise on Christmas Day musicians climb to the belfry of the church and play four hymns, one to each point of the compass. The first is "A Mighty Fortress Is Our God." As they finish, the church bells begin to ring and the "peace of Christmas" is ushered in. The holiday continues with feasting and merriment until Epiphany.

During the Christmas season of 1903 Einar Holbøll, a Danish postal clerk, conceived the idea of asking people to buy a special Christmas stamp while the holiday spirit of giving was strong. He thought that just a penny on every letter would help to bring in money to help sick and needy children. Other citizens became interested in the idea, and they joined him in making plans. The reigning king, Christian IX, gave his approval to the plan to sell the sticker for the smallest monetary unit, and the first issue bore the likeness of the late Queen Louise. From December 6 to January 6, 1904, the first Christmas seals for the prevention of tuberculosis were sold in Denmark, and over four million were sold that year. Einar Holbøll died in 1927, and that Christmas he was honored by his portrait on the Danish seal of the year. He had lived to see his idea travel around the world; by the time of his death forty-five countries had adopted the plan.

Another Danish idea reaches beyond the boundaries of the country—the Danish Christmas plates, which Denmark has given to the world as a Christmas keepsake for more than fifty years. The blue and white colors are symbolic of the season—white for purity and blue a symbol of heaven and the Virgin Mary. The porcelain plates show scenes associated with Christmas, such as "the arrival of the Christmas train," or "delivering Christmas letters."

PINE-CONE ELF

MATERIALS:

> wooden cone 4″ high with ½″ bead on top
> pine cone
> paint—red, white, skin-tone
> strip of white fur
> wire

DIRECTIONS:

1. Paint a wooden cone red, with a small elf face on one side. (Cone should be slender—1½″ at base, tapering to ⅛″ at top—and topped by a ½″ wooden bead.) Glue strip of white fur on for beard.
2. Touch the tips of a pine cone with white paint to simulate snow.
3. Glue the elf to the stem end of pine cone and hang to tree by a wire fastened around wooden bead.

PAPER CONE

MATERIALS:

    red or green construction paper
    gold paper
    gold ribbon

DIRECTIONS:

1. From construction paper cut a 7¾" square.
2. Cut a gold paper square measuring 7½". Make shallow scallops 1¾" wide on two sides of the gold square.
3. Glue gold square onto construction paper so that a border of red (or green) shows beyond the gold scallops. Round the corners of the construction paper to follow the gold scallop.
4. Roll the square into a cone, with the scalloped edge at top. Glue overlapping edge. Tie gold ribbon on the top corner for hanging.

WOVEN PAPER HEART

MATERIALS:

    red and white paper

DIRECTIONS:

1. Measure and cut a square of white paper 10¼" x 10¼". Fold in half, then fold in half again.
2. On the edges of the square away from the fold mark of the top of a heart. Cut. There are four hearts on top of each other.
3. On the topmost heart measure four lines ¾" apart from the folded edge toward top of

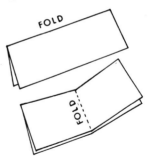

21

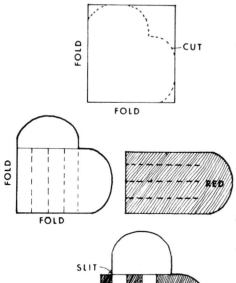

heart. Cut on these lines, leaving the curved part of the heart solid.

4. From red paper cut a piece 3¾″ x 6½″. Cut one end of the red paper in shape of a half-heart, using the full-size heart as pattern. Mark three lines ¾″ apart and cut from the bottom up, leaving the top solid and uncut.

5. Weave the red half-heart into the white heart, over and under. Cut two slits at bottom of white heart for the red ends and fold all the extra length of red inside the heart. Glue curve of red heart to white.

6. Glue or staple the open sides of the heart together to form a basket.

7. Fold a strip of red paper (7″ x 1″) lengthwise and glue together. Attach this to the heart basket for handle.

RAFFIA RING WITH HEARTS

MATERIALS:

raffia (natural color)
red construction paper
wire

DIRECTIONS:

1. Braid raffia around a wire ring 6″ in diameter.

2. Cut eight hearts 2″ wide from red construction paper. Fold hearts in center. Glue four hearts together on center line, making two groups of hearts. Spread open from center.

3. Sew a fine thread through each group of hearts at center point and attach the groups to raffia ring, one above the other.

22

DRINKING-STRAW STAR

MATERIALS:

drinking straws
red thread

DIRECTIONS:

1. Tie twenty drinking straws together at center. (It is easier to do this by tying two groups of ten. Pinch ten straws tightly at center and tie together; then join them to the other bundle of ten.)
2. One inch from center tie the straws together in groups of four, using red thread and tying a tight knot. There will be ten ties.
3. Now take two of the four straws from a group and tie to two of an adjoining group at the outer end of the straws. This will form a ten-pointed star.

GOLD PAPER STAR

MATERIALS:

gold wrapping paper
wire or thread

DIRECTIONS:

1. Cut two stars. If paper is gold on both sides, only one star is necessary.
2. Cut toward center on dotted lines.
3. Place the two stars together, with gold surface outside. Roll each section to a point; staple lower edges together. (Do not flatten the points of the star: the rolled look gives distinction.)
4. Hang from a point by thin wire or thread.

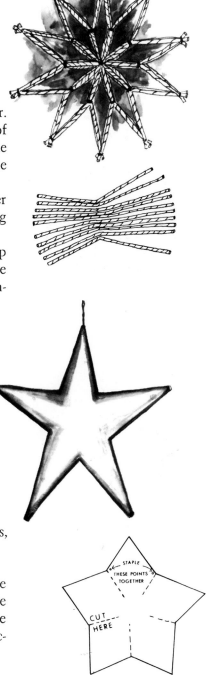

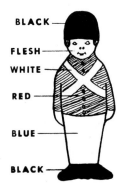

SOLDIER

BLACK
FLESH
WHITE
RED
BLUE
BLACK

MATERIALS:

   ¼″ plywood, 7½″ x 3¾″
   tempera paint—red, white, blue, black, flesh
     tone

DIRECTIONS:

1. Cut soldier from plywood with jigsaw.
2. Draw in design lines. Paint with tempera. Trousers are bright blue, coat red, hat and shoes black. Crossbelt is white, and buttons are black.
3. Make a tiny hole through top of head and hang to tree by wire.

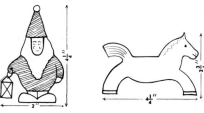

WOODEN CUTOUTS

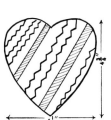

Besides the soldier, other cutouts from ¼″ plywood are: elf, small horse, bird, and large heart (see diagrams).

Paint the horse and bird white with touches of gray. Paint the heart red and decorate with diagonal rows of gold rickrack. Paint the elf's cap bright red, mittens and legs red; paint his shoes black and his clothing gray; make a long white beard almost to bottom of jacket.

YARN DOLL

MATERIALS:

beige yarn
yellow yarn
brown and red cloth
small-patterned cotton material for shirt and
    cap
denim for trousers

DIRECTIONS:

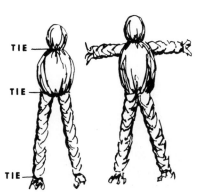

1. Cut 30 lengths of 4-ply beige yarn 20″ long.
   Tie in center and bring ends together.

2. Tie again tightly 2″ from first tying. This
   forms the head. Tie loosely 1½″ down to
   form waist.

3. Divide the yarn into equal parts to form legs.
   Braid the legs and tie at ankle location.

4. With 18 pieces of yarn braid a strip 9″ long
   for arms. Tie at wrist. Run the braided arms
   through the body section.

5. Sew a few strands of bright yellow yarn to
   head for hair. Sew two small brown triangles
   on face for eyes and a small red heart for
   mouth.

6. Make a shirt of cotton and slip over the head.
   Make a pointed cap 3″ high with a tassel of
   beige yarn at peak of cap and sew to head.
   Complete the costume with denim trousers.

7. Hang to tree by a length of beige yarn.

DRUMS

MATERIALS:

shirt cardboard
red wrapping paper
white paper
green ribbon, ¼″ wide
gold braid
white large-headed pins

DIRECTIONS:

1. From shirt cardboard cut a strip 8½″ long and 3″ wide. Join 3″ ends with staples or glue to make a cylinder.
2. Cover the sides with red wrapping paper and the ends with white paper. Use bands of ribbon to cover the joinings.
3. Trim drum with gold braid held in place with large-headed white pins. Run the braid in V's from top to bottom row of ribbon, making a loop at the end for hanging.

DOUBLE HEARTS

MATERIALS:

heavy red paper
green paper
twine

DIRECTIONS:

1. Cut five hearts (3″ across) from heavy red paper. From the center of each cut out a 1½″ heart.
2. Fold the large hearts through the center, tip to tip. Glue the five together on the fold line at the top, at the same time inserting and gluing two green leaves between hearts. Leave lower section unglued.
3. Fold the small hearts through the center and

glue these together with two small green leaves at top.

4. Glue each heart group to an end of a 16″ string and hang, one above the other.

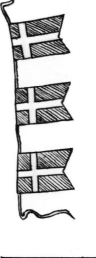

DANISH FLAGS

MATERIALS:

red construction paper
white paper
white wrapping twine

DIRECTIONS:

1. Fold red paper and cut a supply of flags, 3¼″ x 2¼″ (see pattern), placing the 2¼″ measurement on the fold.
2. Glue on the white bars which are ⅜″ wide. Glue bars on each side of fold.
3. Place white twine on the fold line and glue the paper together, so that the string of flags is the same on each side. Place flags on the string two inches apart.

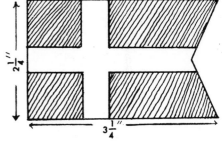

ENGLAND

The idea of a merry Christmas took firm root early in the history of Merrie England, and through the centuries the holiday has been a time of song and feasting.

From early days of British history, Christmas was a special day for rulers and a great day for holding affairs of state. In Saxon England leading nobles gathered at Christmas to advise and counsel the king. William the Conqueror assumed the English throne on Christmas Day, 1066. In the Middle Ages great feasts were ordered by the kings, such as that of Henry III, who had six hundred oxen slaughtered in 1252. Pantomimes, processions, tournaments, and songfests went along with the feasting and the lavish display of dress. In the late Middle Ages costumed maskers, or mummers, began to appear in the English court. Minstrels performed in the court and taverns. Noblemen and gentry often kept a director or master of interludes for yearly entertainments.

Many customs and practices of the English Christmas are linked with ancient pagan ceremonies.

Bringing in the Yule log is a custom with roots more pagan than Christian. Even the name is Scandinavian, for the word "Yule" comes from the word "wheel," indicating the changing of the season as the sun turned in its course. When ancient people celebrated the return of the sun, the lighting of a Yule log was a ceremony of great significance.

Evergreens were brought into houses at the winter solstice, and later on, Christian homes and churches burst into greenery at Christmas time. It is true that the early church forbade the custom, as savoring of paganism, but the practice was too deeply rooted for such prohibition to be effective and in time it was annulled. Gregory the Great wrote in

598 that missionaries should not try to put down pagan customs "upon the sudden" but adapt them "to the praise of God."

The wassail bowl actually originated with the early Norsemen when the beautiful Saxon maiden Rowena presented a bowl of wine to Prince Vorgigen and greeted him "W*aes hael*"—"Be thou well."

The boar's head custom may be connected with ancient rites of pagan times. The pig was eaten during the Scandinavian Yule when the Festival of Lights honored the goddess of plenty, to whom the boar was sacred. At the great medieval Christmas banquets the head was decorated with garlands of rosemary and bay, with an apple or orange thrust between the teeth. Then, to the sound of trumpets, the boar's head was brought in ceremoniously and slowly borne in a processional through the hall on its gold or silver dish. Much more exciting and completely English is the story that the boar's head dinner became a tradition at Queen's College because a wild boar was choked to death by a student who was walking in the woods on Christmas Day reading a copy of Aristotle. When attacked by the boar, the student choked the animal by shoving his book down the throat, then cut off the boar's head to retrieve his book! The boar's head dinner is still observed at Queen's College, where the silver tray with the decorated head is carried by four men, preceded by a chief singer who receives the apple or orange.

Mince pies and plum pudding are distinctly English. The story of plum pudding is that it originated when an English king and his hunting party were lost in a blizzard the day before Christmas. All their meager provisions were put together and tied in a bag to be cooked—meat, flour, apples, eggs, ale, brandy, and sugar. The result was satisfying to the hungry hunters and refined later to become a national dish. The mince pies of the sixteenth century were thought of as edible symbols of the Wise Men because of their spice content. It was a pleasant superstition that whoever ate one such pie on each of the Twelve Days of Christmas would have twelve happy months in the following year. In his diary for Christmas Day, 1666, Samuel Pepys recorded that he rose earlier than his wife "who was desirous to sleep having sat up till four this morning seeing her mayds make mince pies."

Although carol singing began in several European countries in early times, it achieved a great popularity in England, especially in rural areas. Carols were originally simple, happy tunes suggesting dance rhythms rather than the music of hymns. The word "carol" meant a ring dance accompanied by song, and the first carols were secular in theme. The religious carol came into being near the beginning of the fourteenth century as a reaction to church music in Latin. In eighteenth-century England it was often the town "waits" who carried the tunes from door to door, playing upon their instruments. Originally the waits were simply watchmen; later the name was applied to the town musicians who played for processions and civic occasions and who "walked the parish" at Christmas and received rewards from householders where they played. Carol singing still exists, but the singing groups may be choirs collecting for charity or a group of children who are given treats, as were the waits. Adding to the music of the English Christmas are the organized community carol groups and the special carol services in church.

The Christmas tree became popular in England during the reign of Queen Victoria. Actually the tree with which the Queen's husband, German Prince Albert, delighted the royal family in 1841 was not the first tree known in England. In 1832, when she was thirteen, Victoria had recorded in her diary an account of a Christmas tree arranged by her Aunt Sophia. Aunt Sophia's German mother had loved Christmas and had always planned the family celebration around the tree. It was the picture of the Queen and her family, unabashedly sentimental about Christmas, loving their candlelit trees, which appealed to the English. When the *Illustrated London News* in 1848 carried a description of the royal tree, its popularity was assured.

The English Christmas today is one of religious services, family reunions, merry-making, and carol singing. If the massive Yule log is missing, or the boar's head ceremony only practiced at Queen's College, there is still the tradition of the flaming plum pudding, the visit of Father Christmas, and the tree. Children hang up their stockings on Christmas Eve so that Father Christmas can fill them. Midnight church services and special Christmas Day services are held, and the Christmas message of the Queen is broadcast to her people. Christmas dinner is served in early afternoon, and afterward the family gathers around the tree for gifts. Late afternoon tea is served.

Boxing Day is a prolongation of Christmas and is so called from the practice of giving boxes to tenants and tradespeople or to anyone who renders service. This is done on the first weekday after Christmas.

SUGARPLUM BASKET

MATERIALS:

10" plastic doily
wood block, 3½" x 3½"
thumbtacks
gold or silver paint
gold or silver cord

DIRECTIONS:

1. Place doily on wood block and thumbtack to block at center. Fasten the doily to the four sides of block with thumbtacks.
2. Place block and doily in a preheated 350° OPEN oven. As plastic softens, mold and shape sides and corners.
3. Remove from oven and submerge block and basket in a container of ice water until basket hardens. Remove basket from block and staple the corners.
4. When basket is dry, lace silver or gold braided cord through filigree edge of basket, under bottom of basket, and back through other side, extending ends 5" for handle. Tie ends over center of basket.

SUGARPLUMS

MATERIALS:

absorbent cotton balls
red and green spray paint
sugar

DIRECTIONS:

1. Spray cotton balls with paint.
2. Sprinkle with sugar.

CORNUCOPIA

MATERIALS:

shirt cardboard
velvet, brocade, or other rich materials
flowers, lace, and ribbon for trimming
pipe cleaners

DIRECTIONS:

1. Cut a piece of shirt cardboard by pattern. Cut velvet, brocade, or desired material and glue to cardboard, turning under top edge for finished appearance.
2. Form a cone and staple or glue at lapped edge.
3. Trim with lace, ribbon, or flowers, as desired.
4. Cover an 8" pipe cleaner with braid or ribbon and staple to cone.

GUMDROP ORNAMENT

MATERIALS:

gumdrops of different colors
small Christmas bell

DIRECTIONS:

1. Thread needle and tie Christmas bell to end of the thread.
2. String eight gumdrops above the bell, arranging colors attractively.
3. Tie large knot at top and make a small loop for hanging. Put a wire ornament hanger through the loop and hang the gumdrops vertically on the tree.

TAFFETA SWAGS

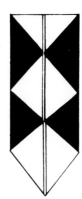

MATERIALS:

red and gold taffeta

DIRECTIONS:

1. Cut strips for swags on the bias of material. For a 12' tree, use strips 6" wide. Add seam allowance of ⅝" to width of strip when cutting. Cut the swag of red taffeta, lining of gold taffeta.
2. With right sides together sew swag and lining together, leaving an opening for turning. Turn and press, then run two rows of basting threads at ends for gathering.
3. For the jabot, cut a red triangle and a matching triangle of gold for lining. Triangles should measure 11" x 11½" x 11½" when finished (see drawing). Add a seam allowance of ⅝" when cutting. Sew the two pieces together, leaving a 2" opening for turning. Turn and press, blindstitch the opening.
4. Mark center of triangle. On each side of center, make two 1" pleats, folding to center and laying one pleat on top of the other. Blindstitch pleats in place across top. Attach to tree by drapery hooks, over gathers of swag section.
5. The number of sections of swags depends on the size of the tree. Cut the top swags to fit the tree; these will be shorter than the bottom ones and must be gauged for individual trees. Attach with drapery hooks.

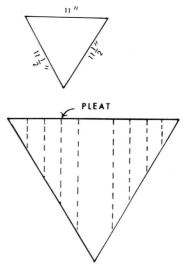

FRENCH
TREE OF
PARADISE

A Paradise tree and the story of Adam and Eve seem a strange way to begin the Christmas season. A look at history, however, gives meaning to both, and the Paradise tree becomes the ancestor of today's Christmas tree.

At an early age the church began to illustrate the Gospel narratives by the use of living pictures accompanied by songs. At Christmas time, for example, the beautiful story of Bethlehem would be made more vivid by placing a manger scene in a corner of the church, with shepherds and Magi at hand. To the Easter and Christmas Mass were added small scenes, or tropes. These interpolations progressed until whole cycles of drama were developed to make the holy-day services more impressive. The miracle and mystery plays thus derived enabled the clergy to present a story in simple dramatic form and to teach the cardinal points of Christianity at a time when there were no printed books and few pictures. The manuscripts of the monasteries were not available to the people.

One of the most popular of the "mysteries" was the Paradise play representing the creation of man, the sin of Adam and Eve, and their expulsion from Paradise. It usually closed with the promise of the coming Savior, and so became a play for the Advent season. The Garden of Eden was indicated by a fir tree hung with apples.

At first the plays were deeply religious in spirit and were presented by the clergy only. The language in which they were written was church Latin, but later they were performed in medieval English, French, and German vernacular. The plays grew in length and number, and the audience grew to such numbers that the churches would not contain them, so the plays were next presented on the steps of the church, finally overflowing to city squares. This resulted in a separation of the plays from the regular service of the church. Worldly, satirical, and humorous elements were inserted. In the Christmas plays, for example, a raging Herod gave comic relief. Once outside the church lay actors took part, and the church prohibited the clergy from appearing in plays outside the church walls. Actors were trained for the stage, as the plays were taken up by guilds and trade unions. Comedy and buffoonery were introduced to such an extent that the sacred drama degenerated into a farce.

The Paradise tree, the only symbolic object of the mystery play of the church, now found its way into the homes of the faithful. In the fifteenth century the custom developed of decorating the Paradise tree, already bearing apples, with small white wafers representing the Holy Eucharist. These wafers were later replaced by little pieces of pastry cut in the shape of stars, angels, flowers, hearts, and bells. And finally other cookies were introduced in the shape of men, birds, dogs, roosters, lions, and other animals. Tradition called for the latter being cut from brown dough while the first group was made of white dough.

GENERAL DIRECTIONS
FOR TREE

The topiary tree should be about 8′ high —with three tiers approximately 1′ apart. Stand tree in jardinière.

Red plastic apples may be purchased at a florist, department store, etc. Tie gold thread around the stems in 8″ lengths. Then tie apples to aluminum hoops—spacing them about 5″ apart and letting them hang down about 6″. Hoops are wired unobtrusively to the underside of each tier of the tree; keep hoops as level as possible so that apples hang evenly. About four dozen apples are needed for a tree of this size.

Use two-tone crepe paper for the roses— red on one side to blend with the apples, pink on other side. Use about six dozen—placing the buds on the top tier and the full-blown 3″ flowers on the bottom tier. Wire snugly to tree, rather thickly.

Use Communion wafers sparingly—about 30, hung at random close against the tree.

WAFERS

MATERIALS:

Communion wafers, 2″ in diameter
rice paper
fine gold thread
clear aerosol plastic

DIRECTIONS:

1. Cover each side of wafer with rice paper, gluing a fine gold-thread loop at the top for hanging.
2. Spray on both sides with clear aerosol plastic.

ROSES

MATERIALS:

"Galaxy" crepe paper (a two-tone, double-weight paper)
#4 knitting needle or pencil
Scotch tape
florist's wire
floral tape

DIRECTIONS:

1. Cut four petals of each of three sizes.
2. Roll each petal, beginning at the tip end, on a #4 knitting needle or pencil.

3. Begin with the smallest petals to form the center of rose. Pleat petals at the bottom, then Scotch-tape them, one at a time, to an 8″ piece of florist's wire. Keep rolled edges turned outward.
4. Form center with four smallest, then add second size evenly around center, then the largest for a full-blown rose. Use only eight petals for the buds.
5. Cover all exposed Scotch tape, petal ends, and wire with green floral tape.
6. Wire roses to tree by their own stems.

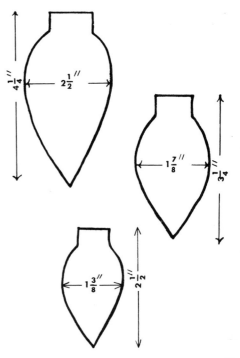

GERMANY

Germany is a nation steeped in Christmas lore, and much of the world's Christmas tradition is of German origin.

Saint Boniface, an English missionary monk, brought Christianity to Germany about A.D. 700. On Christmas Eve, according to tradition, he came upon a group of worshipers who had gathered to sacrifice the son of their chieftain to the pagan god Thor. The scene of the sacrifice was a mighty oak. Boniface struck one blow against the mighty oak and it immediately toppled in the wind. When the throng about him asked for the word of God, he pointed not to the oak but to an evergreen and bid them take it into their homes as a tree of the Christ Child. The evergreen, he taught, stood for peace, not deeds of blood, and was the sign of endless life, the tree of the Christ Child.

Martin Luther also is credited with the introduction of the Christmas tree. On Christmas Eve, after a walk under the stars, he set up an evergreen tree in his home for his wife and children and lighted it with many candles to symbolize Christ as the Light of the World.

Another beautiful story concerns the poor forester and his family who befriended a child—the Christ Child, who touched a fir tree beside the door of their cottage. This became the first Christmas tree.

Whatever its origin, the Christmas tree was long ago made the symbol of Christmas by the German people, and they have spread its use wherever they have gone. The glass balls and fancy tinsel ornaments are a heritage which the world owes to the Germans.

Saint Nicholas, the fourth-century bishop who was celebrated for his generosity, was the giver of gifts in Germany in the early days of Christianity. Nicholas was represented as riding a white horse when he arrived on his feast day, December 6, bringing gifts for good children. He was accompanied by a small dark servant who brought bundles of rods or switches for the bad children. After the Reformation, German children were taught that their gifts came from the *Christkind*, and Christmas instead of Saint Nicholas Day became the time for gifts. The *Christkind* is not the Infant Jesus but his messenger, who comes to earth at Christmas time; he is generally pictured as a child dressed in white robes, wearing a golden crown and having big golden wings. Candles are placed in the window to light the *Christkind* on his way.

Preparations for Christmas begin weeks ahead in Germany. A large Advent wreath with one candle is hung on the first Sunday in Advent; each Sunday another candle is added, and a paper star is placed on it each day. Bible passages are written on the stars—an Old Testament verse on one side, a New Testament verse on the other. These are memorized by the children.

From December 6, the stores, markets, and bazaars present a festive appearance. One of the most famous and colorful is the *Christkindlemarket* in Nuremberg, founded by merchants and craftsmen three hundred years ago. It is said that the Christ Child came there to buy presents. At the stands one finds glass balls of many colors, woodcarved fairy-tale figures, stars made from straw, cardboard, and metal, and silver and gold foil. A traditional specialty is the Little Prune Man. His feet, legs, and arms are made of prunes and raisins; his body is a large fig, his head a walnut. Another specialty is the Crackling Gold Angel. Once upon a time a dollmaker comforted his wife after the death of a little daughter by making an angel in the image of her child, and nowadays she lives as the Crackling Gold Angel. Even in the smaller towns which have no fair or market, there are trees of all sizes—so many that they scent the air.

At the markets, too, are many kinds of baked goods, some prepared for Christmas time only. The famous German *Lebkuchen* were baked as early as the beginning of the sixteenth century, and toward the end of that century *Stöllen* and *Pfefferkuchen* are mentioned. The baking of cookies in the form of animals, dwarfs, stars, and the like seems to have been general throughout Germany. Many sweetmeats are baked for the tree—such as the *Kringeln*, transparent sugar cookies twisted in figure eights so they hang easily on the tree. The celebrated Lübecker marzipan imitates all kinds of fruits and vegetables so well that people often take them for real.

Everyone in the house is extremely industrious during the Christmas season, and long before, for the old fashion of making something for those you love has not died out. The German home still exhibits every form of handiwork the women and children of the family know how to practice. Every German family has a tree, to which relatives or intimate friends are invited. As a rule, there is one tree lighted with candles and decorated with ornaments of glass and tinsel, sweetmeats, apples, gilded nuts, and a few small toys. Christmas tree ornaments take varied forms, including the bearded face and peaked cap of the pagan Father Thor, Saint Nicholas as a bishop, and the golden-haired angel, *Christkind* or *Kriss Kringle*. The tree is fixed on a stand in the center of a large square table covered with a snow-white cloth, and around the tree the presents are arranged, those for each person grouped separately. When there are several children and plenty of money in a family, each child sometimes has a tree of his own; at any rate he will have his own table covered with presents and things to eat. All the servants have presents, too, and come in when the tree is lighted.

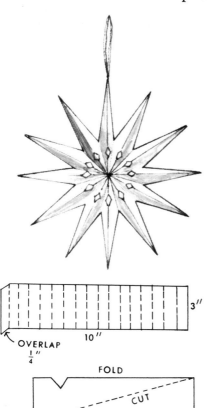

PLEATED PAPER STAR

MATERIALS:

gold paper
string

DIRECTIONS:

1. Cut strip of paper 10¼″ x 3″.
2. Mark off into 1″ divisions. There will be left a ¼″ division for overlap.
3. Carefully fold along drawn lines.
4. Then, with paper tightly folded, draw cutting lines, as illustrated. Draw diagonally from top corner to a point opposite which is 1″ from bottom on the fold. Draw a triangular notch on fold.
5. Cut on drawn lines, through all pleats.
6. Glue the ¼″ lap to the other end of strip.
7. Unfold star by pulling out the points.

8. Cut a gold circle 1½" in diameter and glue to back at center. Attach string for hanging.

BELL

MATERIALS:

square of construction paper, 5¾" x 5¾"
gummed stars, glass beads
glitter

DIRECTIONS:

Always crease on same side of paper and unfold to a square after each step.

1. Fold diagonally and crease sharply from corner to corner. Unfold. Fold and crease diagonally from other two corners. Unfold.
2. Fold straight across center. Unfold. Crease across center from other two sides.
3. Open paper to original square. From a corner bring edge of paper to diagonal line; crease. Bring opposite edge of paper to same diagonal and crease. Your paper will look like a kite.
4. Make "kites" in each corner of the square. This means eight new lines, and the opened square of paper will have this pattern:
5. Push in at center of each edge. This will form a four-pointed star. Pull the points of the star together to make a bell. Push out center.
6. Knot a thread and sew two gummed stars and two glass beads to center point. Fasten. Bring points of star together and sew, leaving thread for hanging.
7. Decorate with glitter.

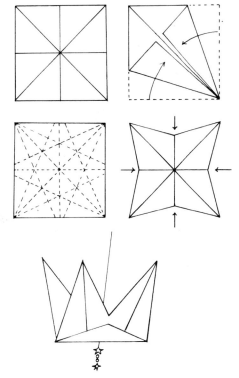

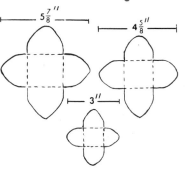

FRINGED BELL

MATERIALS:

construction paper of two colors

DIRECTIONS:

1. Cut one pattern of A and two of B.
2. Fringe the edges of B and glue the fringed flaps to the two largest flaps of A. Glue on underside, so that fringe edges bell.
3. Fold all flaps down on dotted lines.
4. With needle and thread put a string for hanging through the center.
5. Staple smaller flaps together at lowest point.

THREE-BELL CLUSTER

MATERIALS:

construction paper
gummed stars or snowflakes
needle
string
glass beads

DIRECTIONS:

1. Cut three pieces of construction paper as indicated.
2. Fold along dotted lines, and decorate four sides of each bell with gummed stars or snowflakes.
3. Thread a needle and knot string. Push needle through center of square as suspension string.
4. With another needle and thread, go through center of a gummed star and a glass bead;

then sew together the four points of the bell. This will leave star and bead on point of bell.

5. String to make a three-bell cluster.

RIBBON STAR

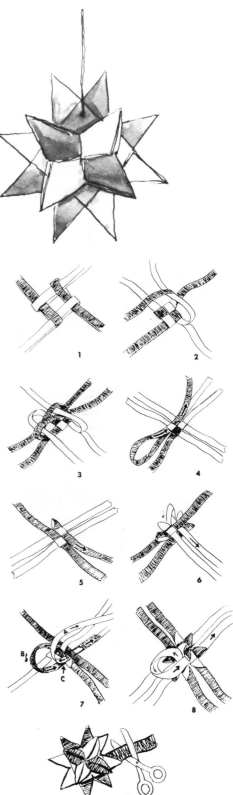

MATERIALS:

> 4 pieces of ribbon, 2 light and 2 dark, ¾" x 24"

DIRECTIONS:

1. Fold 4 pieces of ribbon, 2 light and 2 dark in half. Interlock to form basket weave and pull ends tightly.
2. Lift top ribbons; fold one across the other to form second basket weave.
3. Pull ends tightly.
4. Bring one loose end up and slip it through one open side. Turn loop inside out with thumb and forefinger.
5. Pull end through until loop forms point or triangle when creased (see diagram). Repeat with remaining 3 loose ends. Now you have 4 star points.
6. Turn star over and repeat steps 4 and 5. Now there are 8 star points.
7. To make center standing points, lift and fold back one of the top light-colored strips, A. Take dark strip B and keeping the right side up, loop the strip counterclockwise and slip it into slot C under raised ribbon. Pull through to form a point at C.
8. Repeat procedure with remaining top strips to make 4 standing points. Turn star over and repeat steps 7 and 8.
9. Trim extending ribbons.

From Listaite and Hildebrand, *A New Look at Christmas Decorations*, p. 11.

HOLLAND

The story of Christmas in Holland begins with the story of Saint Nicholas, a Christian bishop of the fourth century who was known for his generous deeds and kindly acts.

Saint Nicholas was born in Asia Minor and became a bishop while he was still a young man. He was the patron saint of boys, young men, and sailors in Greece and Sicily and in many other places. His fame spread to Russia, Europe, and to Lapland; Russian peasants especially loved him because he protected the weak and poor. Many churches were named for him, and countless legends arose concerning his good deeds. One of the best-known legends is of his generosity to an impoverished nobleman who lacked dowries for his three daughters. The kindly saint dropped three bags of gold through the window. One of the bags landed in a stocking by the fireside, so the custom developed of hanging up stockings for the visit of Saint Nicholas, whose feast day is December 6. Dutch children set their shoes beside the fireplace.

Along the way Saint Nicholas acquired a helper or assistant who carries the birches or willows which punish bad children. In Holland the helper is called Black Peter.

Long ago Saint Nicholas was chosen by the people of the Netherlands as the patron saint of children. The arrival of the generous saint on December 5 (Saint Nicholas Eve) marks the beginning of the holiday season in Holland.

Saint Nicholas is the patron saint of Amsterdam, and his entrance into that city is colorful and rich with ceremony. Wearing the rich robes and miter of a bishop, he arrives from Spain in a boat filled with gifts. Excitement is high among young and old, as he disembarks amid the shouting of people, the booming of guns, and the ringing of church bells. At the port he mounts his horse and is followed along the street by the mayor and other dignitaries. (Other port cities enjoy similar visits.) Black Peter, his Moorish helper, accompanies Saint Nicholas, and he wears the puffed velvet breeches and plumed beret of sixteenth-century Spain.

During the weeks before December 5, Saint Nicholas has listened at doors and chimneys to learn if the children are good. Now he questions them about their behavior and promises to leave toys if they have been good. The children place their shoes before the fireplace, and in them put hay and a carrot for the horse, cookies and candy for the saint.

Gifts are exchanged in Holland on Saint Nicholas Day as "surprises," each gift accompanied by a bit of verse and signed *"Sinter Klass."* The giver of a gift does not strive for a beautifully wrapped present, but works hard to camouflage it, and with his rhyme tries to remain anonymous. The greater the talent of the giver, the more fun for the recipient and the friends who attend the party.

At Christmas time every family has a tree, and the house is decorated with greens and holly. However, it is not a time for parties. Christmas Eve and Christmas morning are devoted to church services. Family gatherings, with stories and carols, mark the afternoon, and at seven there is a feast. Musical performances in churches, concert halls, on radio, and at school honor the Christ Child throughout the season.

PINWHEELS

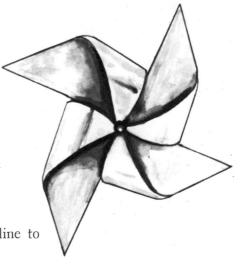

MATERIALS:

two-color heavy decorator foil
small Christmas tree ball
5" green pipe cleaner

DIRECTIONS:

1. Cut a 6" square of foil.
2. From each corner cut on a diagonal line to one inch of center.

53

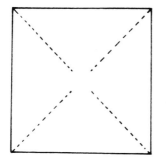

3. Staple every other point to center. Run a pipe cleaner through center and glue a small Christmas tree ball on the end to decorate pinwheel. Use the end of pipe cleaner on back side for hanging.
4. Make a 12" star for top of the tree in the same way.

COOKIES

INGREDIENTS:

1 cup sugar
⅝ cup shortening
1 egg
1 pint molasses or honey
½ pound citron, finely chopped
6 cups of flour
1½ teaspoons soda
1 teaspoon anise seed (optional)
1 teaspoon anise powder (optional)
½ teaspoon cloves
½ teaspoon nutmeg
1 teaspoon cinnamon
½ teaspoon cardamon or ½ teaspoon coriander
¾ cup buttermilk or sour milk
½ cup chopped nuts

DIRECTIONS:

1. Cream sugar and shortening. Stir in beaten egg, molasses, and citron.
2. Sift together the flour, soda, and spices. Add dry ingredients to the molasses mixture alternately with milk.
3. Stir in nuts and store overnight in refrigerator.
4. Roll out to ¼" thickness. Cut in a variety of shapes and bake in 375° oven for 10 minutes.

5. *Kerstkransjes* (wreathlike cookies to be plucked off the Christmas tree by children) may be made by this recipe. Yield: dozens of cookies.

OTHER ORNAMENTS

Pine Cones

Various sizes, sprayed silver and wired for hanging.

English Walnuts

Sprayed gold and wired. Open shell slightly at top and glue in the wire.

Fruits

Wire apples, oranges, and tangerines with florist's wire. Fresh fruit will last about a week, depending on temperature of room. If tree is near a heater, fruits deteriorate quickly.

Sugar Bells

White sugar bells with red trim from bakery.

Candles

Three-inch candles, red or white, in silver holders.

Chocolates

Various shapes of Dutch chocolates in foil wrappings.

Beads

Strings of glass beads, in silver and red.

ITALY

In Italy the Christmas season lasts for three weeks, beginning eight days before Christmas and ending with Twelfth Night. The Christmas celebrations center around the birth of the baby Jesus, and a *presèpio*, or manger, is prepared in every home. Members of the family offer prayers and light candles every morning. As a result of this concentration on the significance of Christmas, Italy has not adopted the Christmas tree to any extent, and the joviality of the Northern holiday is absent.

The manger scene which emphasizes the meaning of Christmas was originated by Saint Francis of Assisi. In the village of Greccio in 1223 he arranged a manger with hay. Using live animals and the people of the village, he depicted the scene at Bethlehem in such a way that the people with their own eyes could see the privation suffered by the Holy Family. Saint Francis arranged for Mass to be celebrated at this Nativity scene. Many people came to Greccio, along with the brothers of Saint Francis, and the songs and service around the crib filled their hearts with joy at the renewing of the mystery of the Nativity.

Following Saint Francis, manger scenes were set up in churches, and people brought gifts to the Holy Infant. Later the crib became the inspiration of artists and craftsmen who made miniature scenes for their own homes. The popularity of this custom spread to the court, and nobles and kings hired artists to produce lavish scenes. Many figures were added representing various social classes, all clad in the dress of the day. Always the *presèpio* in the Italian home has been the center of interest, and the figures are carefully treasured. Some are generations old and perhaps handmade by a member of the family. The Nativity scene appears also in shop windows, in windows of houses, and even in open doorways.

Frequently the manger scene, laid out in the shape of a triangle, is the base for the *ceppo*, a light wooden frame arranged as a pyramid. Several tiers of shelves are supported by the framework, and the whole structure is decorated with colored paper and gilded pine cones, with candles at the corners of the shelves. The shelves above the crib scene hold candy, fruit, or small presents. In some homes there is a *ceppo* for each child in the family. The *ceppo* is in the tradition of the Tree of Light which became the Christmas tree in other countries. It is thought that it originated as a substitute for the Yule Log and that the pyramidal form represents the flames.

During the Italian Advent season, shepherds come into towns and villages from the hillsides, saluting with their music the shrines of the Virgin and Child which adorn the streets. The costume of the shepherds is picturesque—goat-skin trousers, flaming red vest, a bright blue coat, broad-brimmed felt hat with peacock feathers and a red tassel. The instruments of these *pifferari* are similar to bagpipes. Before each shrine the shepherds pipe their sweet music to the Holy Child and pause before carpenter shops in honor of Joseph. From house to house they go, asking if Christmas is to be kept there. If the master says it is, a wooden spoon is left to mark the place. Later they will return to sing Nativity songs:

"On that blessed night
When Jesus Christ was born
So brightly shone the star above
'Twas radiant as the morn."

Christmas Eve is a family affair. Although no particular dish is common to all Italy, the festive supper lasts for several hours until it is time to go to church at midnight. Fowl and fish, a delicately prepared dish of eels, a pastry filled with cheese, and a candy called *torrone* are some of the dishes served. Christmas Day is also a sacred day and a time for church attendance.

The urn of fate is an Italian tradition, a gay and happy part of the Christmas time. The urn is a large ornamental bowl or crock which holds wrapped presents for members of the family. Each takes a turn until all the presents are distributed. Many of the presents are empty boxes; everyone is sure to draw a blank before getting his present, but this adds more suspense and merriment.

For the children the gift-giving occasion is Epiphany, January 6.

Formerly, on the Eve of Epiphany, the children placed their shoes on the hearth. The modern custom is to hang up a stocking in anticipation of the visit of Befana, the only figure in the Italian Christmas who can be compared to Santa Claus. Befana is not "a right jolly old elf," however, but a woman of stern nature and forbidding appearance. Her arrival is announced by a bell, and little children in Italy who hear a bell ringing on the Eve of Epiphany are told to hurry off to sleep before Befana comes.

Befana's name is probably derived from the name of the feast day, Epiphany, and her story is similar to that of the Russian Babouschka. The folk tale says that Befana was asked by the Wise Men for directions to Bethlehem. They explained to her their mission and asked her to accompany them, but she declined because of her household duties. Later a shepherd appeared and asked her to go to Bethlehem, but she again said no. When it was dark, a great light in the heavens and a band of angels brought to Befana the realization of her mistake, and she rushed out to join the Wise Men. Befana was too late to find the Christ Child, and now goes about on the Eve of Epiphany leaving gifts for the sleeping children of Italy.

CEPPO

MATERIALS:

> ¾" plywood
> 3 closet rods, 4′ 3″
> ¾" screen molding
> 1 box 1″ brads
> 1½" nails
> wood glue
> light blue flat paint
> antiquing glaze in Wedgewood blue
> clear glazing liquid
> umber
> 4 sheets gift-wrap paper
> 12 bayberry candles (8″)

DIRECTIONS:

1. The *ceppo* is 4' tall. The four triangular shelves are equilateral and measure 29", 23", 17", and 11".
2. Drill holes in corners of shelves and run closet rod through holes, making shelves approximately 12" apart. Small finishing toppiece is 6½" and 6" above top shelf.
3. Glue and brad the molding to edges of shelves and toppiece.
4. Hammer nails up through all corners of the 4 shelves. These will serve as candle holders.
5. Paint *ceppo* with 2 coats of flat blue paint and allow to dry. Antique with Wedgewood blue.
6. Cut decorative paper in triangles measuring 21", 15", and 9". Center papers and glue to bottom three shelves. Mellow paper with umber in clear glazing liquid. Apply lightly and wipe off.
7. Place candles on nails.

STAINED GLASS WINDOW

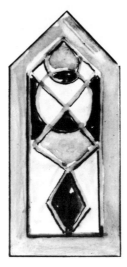

MATERIALS:

    piece of glass, 5" wide and 10½" from base to apex
    lead tape
    lead adhesive
    glass stain in purple, rose, blue, and amber
    thinner for stain

DIRECTIONS:

1. With lead tape work out a design for window, as desired.
2. Apply lead adhesive to lead tape and press the tape into place on the glass.

3. Paint glass as desired, using glass stain.
4. Mount the window on *ceppo* shelf on a display card holder.

CRÈCHE

MATERIALS:

¼" plywood, 11" x 8"
½" dowel, 24" long
match stick blind, 14" x 11"
walnut stain
clear glazing liquid
umber
wax metallics
1" brads
wood glue
crèche figures

DIRECTIONS:

1. Cut two 8" pieces from dowel and two 4" pieces.
2. Attach 8" posts to corner on long side of plywood with brads and attach 4" posts to other corners.
3. Glue matchstick blind to posts. Stain with walnut stain.
4. Stain inexpensive crèche figures with clear glaze and umber. Allow to dry. Brush and wipe with wax metallics.

FRUIT DECORATIONS

MATERIALS:

15 small artificial fruit clusters
2 bunches small grapes
1 small pineapple
5½ yards hot pink velvet ribbon
Medici color glaze
13½ yards small gold roping
florist's wire
wax metallics

DIRECTIONS:

1. Lightly brush and wipe fruit in Medici glaze. Allow to dry.
2. Brush and wipe fruit with wax metallics for jewel-tone antique finish.
3. Wire fruit and attach to candles, using two clusters on each corner of the bottom shelf. Add velvet bows, allowing approximately 14" for each.
4. Place grapes, pineapple, remaining fruit clusters and bows on top piece.
5. Swag gold roping, using brads to secure.

LITHUANIA

Christmas Eve is one of the most important family holidays of the Lithuanians. It is a day of peace, good will, religious recollection, and intimate family reunion. Members of the family fast all day as they prepare for *Kucia*, the Christmas Eve dinner, highlight of the day, and for *Kaledos*, Christmas Day.

The home is cleaned thoroughly, and holiday foods fill the house with tantalizing aromas. After the chores are done, members of the family scrub in the *pirtis* (steam bath) and don holiday garb. The Christmas Eve table is spread with sweet fresh hay and covered with a handloomed snowy linen cloth reserved for the occasion. A crucifix and a plate of holy wafers are placed in the center of the table. When the evening star appears in the sky, the head of the family begins the meal with a prayer of thanksgiving for past blessings and a wish that the family remain intact during the coming year. He breaks and shares the holy wafers with each member of the family, and they, in turn, with each other.

The Christmas Eve menu consists of twelve courses which commemorate the twelve Apostles, but no meat is served. Soup, fish, vegetables, a small hard biscuit served with poppy-seed and honey sauce, and an oatmeal pudding are included. The meal is leisurely, and conversation centers on the significance of Christmas.

In some sections of Lithuania the *Kucia* table is not cleared of food, lest the Christ Child and his Mother visit during the night. It is also believed that souls of deceased members of the family might return briefly—and they must find a hospitable table. The floor is carefully swept so there will not be even a crumb on which a visitor might stumble.

Christmas Eve is a time when old superstitions foretelling the future are enjoyed. Straws are drawn from under the tablecloth to determine the length of life—or in the case of young people, the length of their single life. The future can be seen in the shape of molten lead, wax, or fat poured into cold water. On Lithuanian farms children run frequently to the well to taste the water, for legend says that it changes into wine on this night; or they run to the barn to capture the mystic moment when the animals have the power to speak.

The hay from under the tablecloth, together with choice bits of *Kucia* food, is given to animals in gratitude for their work and in appreciation of the thought that animals in the stable guarded and warmed the Holy Child at Bethlehem. The family makes every effort to attend the Shepherd's Mass at midnight or at dawn.

Christmas Day is spent in feasting and merry-making. Young people make rounds of visits. Folk songs and Christmas carols, vigorous folk dances and holiday food, cider and ale, characterize the celebration. Christmas trees, if used, are decorated with geometric ornaments of straw.

Beside the Christmas tree is placed a cradle into which each member of the family places a straw for every kind deed or gracious word during the holidays.

BIRD CAGE

MATERIALS:

9 pieces of reed 13" long
wire
red twine
1 milkweed pod
red felt

DIRECTIONS:

1. Soak the reed so that it is pliable. Fasten the 9 pieces together, wiring at both ends. Cover wire with red twine, and at one end make a 2" loop for hanging.

2. Spread the reeds apart at the center to form a cage. Place a 4" wire circle inside the cage at center to hold the reeds in place. Tie wire to reed with red thread, then cover the wire circle by crocheting around it with heavy red thread.
3. Make the bird of a milkweed pod and red felt. Cut a head of red felt and glue it into a slit at the top of the pod. Glue a red felt wing to each side.
4. Make feet for the bird by slitting a 1" length of reed into three pieces at one end, like toes, then push the other end of the reed into the body of bird.
5. Hang the bird in center of cage by a double red thread, tied at top of cage and knotted inside the body of the bird.

TEARDROP AND ELF

MATERIALS FOR TEARDROP:

3 pieces of reed, approximately 30" long
several lengths of raffia
small strip of red felt
masking tape

DIRECTIONS:

1. Cut 3 pieces of reed 30" long. Lay flat on table, bending to form teardrop shape. Fasten ends together with masking tape. Loop should be about 9" x 12".
2. Soak raffia in water. Thread tapestry needle with wet raffia. Weave between and around the 3 pieces of reed until teardrop is covered with raffia. Tie ends of raffia on back side.
3. At top, sew back and forth with raffia through the masking tape to secure. Wrap ends with raffia to give a finished look.

4. Tie red felt in one knot, cut ends at angle, and sew to top of teardrop.

Materials for Elf:

1 piece of copper wire 14″ long
1 piece of copper wire 5″ long
cotton
1 red bead and 2 black beads
scrap of nylon hose
red felt
small piece of natural-colored burlap
wire

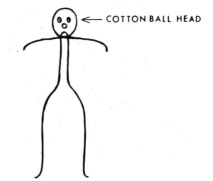

Directions:

1. Bend 14″ length of copper wire in half, shaping for body and legs. Secure 5″ length across body for arms.
2. Sew cover of nylon hose over cotton ball and fasten to top of wire frame for face. Make eyes of white felt with black bead in center. Make nose of red bead or use tiny piece of red nylon stuffed with cotton for nose.
3. Wire cotton to frame for body. Now cut a strip of red felt, 2½″ wide. Fold, stitch, and turn. Cut in small lengths (about 6″ for legs and 4″ for arms). Rip back enough seam to pull the legs up onto body in the back and in the front. Sew together from crotch upward. Rip arm seams and pull onto body and sew together.
4. Cover center of body with a strip of felt approximately 1½″ x 5″. Sew ends together in back.
5. Cut a piece of burlap 3″ x 6″ for apron. Fringe edges, about ⅜″. Cut hole in center and slip over the head of elf. Tie around body with red felt or cord.
6. Cut a triangle of red felt for hat (see pattern). Fold the felt, stitch triangle on the long side. Turn. Sew a raffia tassel on peak of hat, fold

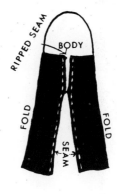

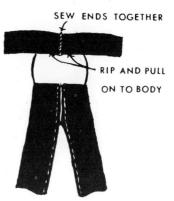

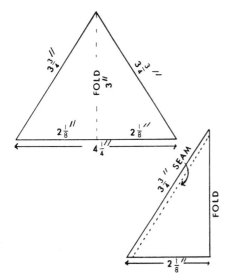

the peak down ½″ and sew to front of hat. Sew hat to elf's head.

7. Tie raffia around wrists. Cut small piece of burlap (about 1½″ x 3″). Fold edges together and sew to feet of elf, turning up the toes.
8. Glue on a cotton beard.
9. Braid threads of burlap to make a cord 12″ long. Sew burlap cord to elf at back of neck and back of cap and to the top of the teardrop, making a 3″ loop for hanging.

CHAIN

MATERIALS:

    reed
    wire
    red twine

DIRECTIONS:

For each section cut 2 pieces of reed 5″ long; wire together at ends. Cut a piece of reed 12″ long; soak; then make into a 2″ circle, twisting reed around itself. Insert circle into center of loop and wire to sides, twisting wire in opposite directions on each side so that circle will remain firm. Cover all wires with red twine. Begin the next section, linking it to the first.

CROSS

MATERIALS:

    red felt
    raffia
    straw

Cut two red felt crosses, 8½" x 12¼". Glue together, gluing a braided raffia loop between the layers of felt at top. Glue three rows of straw in the center of both the upright and cross beams.

LOOP WITH ANGELS

MATERIALS:

3 pieces of reed 27" long
raffia
36 pieces of straw 12" long, 18 pieces 4" long
4 stalks of bearded wheat
wire
red yarn
3 wooden beads
masking tape

DIRECTIONS:

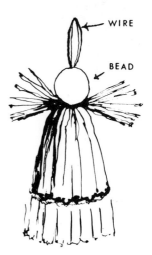

1. Using 3 pieces of reed 27" long, make 3 circles. At the point where ends join slip a paper clip on to strengthen the circle. Fasten ends and paper clip with masking tape.
2. Thread a tapestry needle with wet raffia and weave the reeds together, weaving under one, over the next, and around the third until the circle is covered. At the top of circle tie four pieces of wheat, two on each side, using raffia to hold the wheat and to cover any exposed masking tape.
3. For each angel use 12 pieces of wet straw 12" long. Fold in center; twist wire around center, bringing wire through bead at top.
4. Use 6 pieces of wet straw 4" long for wings. Pinch together in center and wire. Spread the straw, then weight with a heavy object until

dry. When dry, wire to body, covering wire with raffia.

5. Place a circle of wire around the skirt so that the straw stands out. With red yarn weave around the skirt with one row of backstitch, covering the wire which holds skirt in position.

6. Wire wings to body and cover the wire with raffia. Hang the angels in the circle on a wire, with an angel at each end of wire and one in the center.

WHISK-BROOM ANGEL

MATERIALS:

1 large whisk broom
1 styrofoam ball
natural-colored burlap and wooden beads
small reeds
scraps of red wool, black felt, red felt
wheat
red rickrack and ball fringe
wire

DIRECTIONS:

1. For body, cut threads where whisk broom is stitched. Cover with water, add cup of clorox. Soak overnight in clorox solution, then dry.

2. For halo, use reed or long matchsticks. Weave around outer edge with red heavy double thread, putting stick between thread, then thread through wooden bead, then outside of next stick, etc.

3. For head, cut styrofoam ball in half and scoop out inside to fit whisk broom handle. Cover the two pieces with nylon hose and glue to inside. Fit halo between two sections of ball; glue ball together, with broom handle, halo,

and nylon overlap inside. Weight, and leave overnight to dry. Cut nose and lashes of black felt and a red-felt oval mouth. Glue to face.

4. Cut two thicknesses of natural burlap for each wing, stitch close to edge, and wire around edge to hold shape. Glue a 1″ fringe of burlap around wings and cover raw edges and wire with red rickrack, allowing fringe to extend beyond rickrack. Wire wings together and wire to back of whisk broom.

5. Cut outer layer of broom to shape of cape and weave red ball fringe around it. Wrap neck with a short piece of red fringe. Make a bow of red wool yarn, with streamers, and tie in front of cape.

6. Tape bearded wheat underneath dress for a lacy effect. Glue bearded wheat to sides and back of head to hang down for hair.

SUNBURST STAR

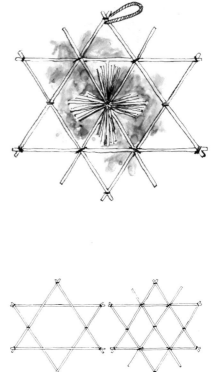

MATERIALS:

8 pieces of reed, 7½″ long
14 pieces of straw, 4″ long
red twine
fine wire

DIRECTIONS:

1. Make two equilateral triangles from reeds, 7½″ long, wiring ends together. Place one triangle on top of the other to make a six-pointed star. Tie with red twine. Now place two reeds together, crossing them in center of star. Tie these twice at top and twice at bottom.

2. For sunburst, lay 7 pieces of wet straw, 4″ long, on a flat surface. Pinch at center and wire together. Trim ends. Repeat with 7 more pieces. Wire the two bunches together, one

73

held vertically and the other horizontally. Wire to center of star and cover wire with raffia. Attach a red twine to one point of the star for hanging.

SUNBURST

MATERIALS:

10 pieces of stiff straw cut different lengths, 4″, 5″, 6″, 7″, 8″
piece of red yarn 12″ long
round red ¾″ wooden bead

DIRECTIONS:

1. Soak straw in water. Pinch straw together tightly at center and tie with twine. Tie yarn over twine, leaving equal lengths of yarn.
2. Arrange straws in a sunburst pattern. Glue the center to hold the pieces in position.
3. Slip wooden bead on one end of the yarn and knot yarn to hold it. Loop the other piece of the yarn for hanging.

SEEDPOD TEARDROPS

MATERIALS:

red yarn
6 stalks of bearded wheat 8″ long
1 piece of reed 12″ long
round red ¾″ wooden bead
3 half sections of milkweed pods

DIRECTIONS:

1. Push reed through the center of each pod. Arrange the pods about 3″ apart along the

middle of the reed and glue in place. Glue red bead to the bottom of the reed.

2. Wire wheat stalks together, with 3 heads on each side.
3. Wire top of reed to center of wheat spray, so that the reed hangs down from the spray.
4. Make a bow of red yarn by wrapping several strands of yarn around a 5″ piece of cardboard. Slide yarn off and tie at center with a 10″ piece of yarn.
5. Wire bow to the center of wheat spray.
6. Tie ends of the 10″ piece of yarn together and make a loop for hanging.

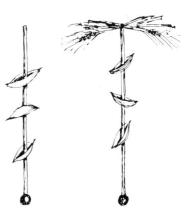

STAR WITH RED FELT CENTER

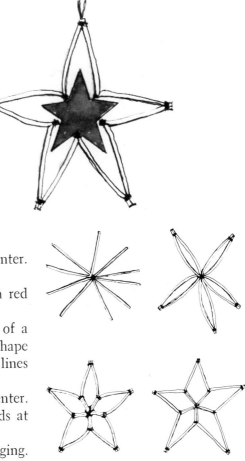

MATERIALS:

5 pieces of reed 12″ long
red felt
red yarn
wire

DIRECTIONS:

1. Soak reeds, then bend each piece at center. Wire the 5 pieces together at center.
2. Wire ends together and cover wire with red yarn.
3. About 1¼″ from center, wire one reed of a section to a reed of adjoining section. Shape the curved lines of the reeds into straight lines forming a 5-pointed star.
4. Make two 4″ stars of red felt to cover center. Place one under and one on top of reeds at center and glue together.
5. Attach red yarn to point of star for hanging.

PIONEER AMERICA

Today, when millions of Christmas tree lights shine forth from windows of homes and the whole nation celebrates the season with a tree as a symbol of Christmas, it is surprising to learn that the tree has not always been a part of the American Christmas scene.

Christmas itself had a hard time in Colonial New England, where the Puritans forbade any observance of the season and even worked harder on Christmas Day than on others to show their disdain for it as a pagan holiday. In 1659 in Massachusetts the Puritan ban on all Christmas celebrations was enforced by this decree: "Whosoever shall be found observing any such day as Christmas or the like, either by forbearing of labour, feasting, or any other way, upon any such accounts as aforesaid, every such person so offending shall pay for every such offense five shillings, as a fine to the county."

The Germans and Moravians of Pennsylvania, however, enjoyed and practiced the customs of their homeland, and the jolly Dutch in New York welcomed Saint Nicholas on his feast day, December 6, and celebrated Christmas with a long holiday. In fact, the city fathers on December 14, 1654, ordered that there should be no more meetings of their board until three weeks after Christmas, since the winter and the holidays were at hand.

In the South, Christmas was a season to be enjoyed with feasting, visiting, hunts, and balls, and with religious devotion. The Christmas tree was not a part of the festive holiday, although evergreen decorations appeared in homes and churches.

There is no documentary evidence to support the story that Hessian soldiers were indulging in a feast around their Christmas tree when Washington surprised them on Christmas Eve, 1776, and won a victory which turned the tide of the war, but the story is told that the General took advantage of the celebrants. The Hessians, far from home, are credited with introducing the tree to children of Newport, Rhode Island.

After the Revolution the Christmas tree began to make its appearance throughout the country. In Pennsylvania, German settlers and Lutheran ministers introduced the tree early in the century, and by 1840 it was more or less common there. The Christmas tree appeared in Boston, Massachusetts, in 1832 when a political refugee from Germany "dressed" a tree for his son. The refugee, Charles Follen, taught German at Harvard and married into a Boston family. His wife recorded that no pains were spared in making the tree as beautiful as possible. In Williamsburg, Virginia, the scholarly Charles Minnegerode delighted friends and townspeople with their first Christmas tree. In Richmond a German storekeeper, August Bodeker, brought joyful amazement to his customers and friends when he set up a tree in his store. Wherever the Christmas-keeping Germans went, there was the tree also!

In the deep South the Swedish singer Jenny Lind met with true hospitality when she arrived in Charleston, South Carolina, at Christmas, 1850, and found that a brilliant Christmas tree had been erected for her. And in Mississippi the tree was introduced in the Vicksburg area by a young matron, Mrs. James Roach, a niece of Jefferson Davis, who had a tree for her children in 1851. The Christmas diary of Mahala Eggleston Roach says: "The children had such a number of gifts that I made a Christmas tree for them; Mother, Aunt and Liz came down to see it; all said it was something new to them. I never saw one but learned from some of the German stories I had been reading." There is no description of ornaments, but the diary for 1852 records that the tree was improved.

What of the decorations for the early trees in America? The Follen tree in Boston has been described in detail: There were wax tapers on every branch, carefully placed so as to light the tree perfectly but not to set fire to anything. Baskets of sugarplums, gilded egg cups, gay paper cornucopias filled with sweets, smart dolls, and other whimsies glittered in the evergreen branches. There was not a twig which had not something sparkling on it. This was the tree which inspired the prediction, "I have little doubt the Christmas tree will become one of the most flourishing exotics of New England."

As the new nation expanded to the West, the Christmas tree appeared with the settlers. A captain in the army set up a tree at Fort Dearborn, Michigan, in 1804. He had learned the custom from the Hessian mercenaries of the Revolution. In Wooster, Ohio, August Imgard, a young German tailor, decorated a tree for his nieces and nephews in 1847, and is honored today at Christmas when a tree is placed at his tomb. A visitor to Texas in 1846 reported seeing a Christmas tree there where scarcely two years before the campfires of Indians were burning. Magazine illustrations at the end of the century depicted cowboys, trappers, and miners celebrating Christmas nostalgically and noisily in bunkhouses or camps.

In the remote cabins where pioneering settlers lived, far from cities and seaports, the smart dolls and other whimsies were lacking, and Christmas was often a make-do event. Toys were often handmade, and decorations were of materials gathered in the woods and fields. A new pair of mittens or socks was a precious gift when women had to spin and dye the yarn they used for knitting. Many a woman who loved pretty things fashioned a doll of corn shucks or used bits of calico to make a granny doll for a child. Gingerbread cookies pleased both children and tree decorator, giving a note of authenticity—though it is probable that many had never heard that cookies in many shapes had decorated German trees for centuries. If pine cones and nuts remained brown instead of being gilded, there was the sweet fragrance of evergreen branches. And to the tree young children brought eager spirits and empty hands which made the simplest tree a wondrous thing.

CORN HUSK DOLL

MATERIALS:

    corn husks
    string
    corn silk
    paint—brown, black, red

DIRECTIONS:

1. Dampen the husks so they will be pliable.
2. Roll a small piece of husk into a ball for the head and another for the upper part of the body. Pin the two balls together, then place a flat piece of husk over them from front to back. Tie a string between the two balls to form neck; tie at waist.
3. For a female doll, make a skirt of several husks and tie to the body at the waist. Trim the skirt evenly at hemline. Make arms of narrow strands of husks, tying at the end to indicate wrist. Glue arms to the body in back. Cut a pinafore and slip over the head, and tie at the waist; or drape a wide shawl around the shoulders and tie down at waist. Paint on a face; braid hair of corn silk and glue in place.

4. For a male doll cut overalls of husk and slip over the arms. Fashion a wide-brimmed hat of husks. Add a spade, with a handle of twisted husk and a flat piece of husk for spade.
5. Corn-husk angels may be made by following these directions and using wings instead of arms. Choose light-colored husks. For a halo, twist a length of husk; glue it to the back of body and head, and end it in a circle above the head.

POMANDER BALL

MATERIALS:

    medium-sized apple
    box of whole cloves
    string or yarn

1. Beginning at top of the apple, press the stems of cloves into apple until it is thickly covered.
2. Place the clove-studded apple in a paper or plastic bag with a small quantity of powdered cinnamon and shake gently until well covered.
3. Fruit will harden in about a week and keep its spicy odor indefinitely.
4. Tie yarn or string around the ball and hang on tree.

YARN DOLL

MATERIALS:

> white or light beige yarn
> yellow yarn
> black and red sewing thread

DIRECTIONS:

1. Cut 30 or 40 pieces of yarn, 10″ long. The amount depends on weight of the yarn.
2. Lay the pieces together lengthwise and tie tightly at the center. Fold and bring the ends together evenly.
3. Tie tightly 1″ from top to form a head.
4. To make the arms, wrap yarn around a 3″ piece of cardboard, wrapping 10 or 12 times. Remove the circle thus formed and tie the ends of yarn. Twist the yarn circle several times to give it a solid appearance, then place it between the two sections of the yarn body just below the head.

5. Tie body to form a waistline. Allow ends of yarn to hang loose for skirt.
6. Sew on yellow yarn for hair. Finish face by sewing black thread for eyes and nose, red thread for mouth.

YARN RINGS

MATERIALS:

Rubber jar rings or cardboard rings
Yarn of dark wine, indigo, or coffee color

DIRECTIONS:

Wrap rings with yarn, making hanger of yarn
loop.

ACORN CLUSTER

With a ⅛" bit, drill holes in acorns. Pour glue
into hole and punch yarn in with a nail.
Tie in clusters of three. Black walnuts may
be used similarly.

POPCORN STRINGS

String unseasoned popcorn on dental floss.
Do not make strings more than 3 feet long,
to avoid tangling. Tie together when length
is needed.

SUGAR COOKIES

Use a basic sugar cookie recipe, sprinkling
cookies with granulated sugar to give a little
glitter. Before baking make a hole with an ice
pick in the cookie for a yarn hanger to be
attached.

GINGERBREAD MAN

Cut a gingerbread man about 6" long. Draw
a face design and mark wrists and feet before
baking. Decorate with raisins only—two for
eyes and two for buttons at waist. Make hole
for hanger before baking.

OLD
RUSSIA

In Old Russia the Christmas celebration began with the appearance of the first evening star on Christmas Eve, when the Advent fast was over. Church services three times a day for six weeks preceded the holiday, and on Christmas Eve there was a long midnight Mass. During the forty-day period of Advent no meat was served, and on the day before Christmas there was no food at all until the first evening star appeared in the sky.

It is not surprising to find the name of Saint Nicholas in the story of the Russian Christmas, for love of the kind and generous bishop spread throughout the Christian world. When Vladimir the Great was baptized at Constantinople, almost one thousand years ago, and made Christianity the religion of his house and of the Russian people, Saint Nicholas was chosen as the patron saint of Russia. For centuries his feast day on December 6 was celebrated with devotion. Saint Nicholas was especially loved by the Russian peasants as protector of the weak and poor against the strong and rich. In days gone by no Russian seaman would weigh anchor without an ikon of Saint Nicholas in the forecastle. Children were told that Nicholas always placed wheat cakes on the window sill for them on Christmas Eve, to be eaten on Christmas Day.

On Christmas Eve it was common for the priest to visit the homes of his communicants, accompanied by boys carrying a vessel of holy water. The priest sprinkled a little of the water in each room and blessed the house.

Christmas Eve supper was served on a table with a layer of straw beneath the cloth, symbolizing the bed in the manger. The blessed wafer of peace and good will was divided among family and friends, followed by main dishes of fish and special cakes. After the meal various members of the family paraded about the neighborhood singing carols, dressed in costumes. Peasants visited a nobleman's house for an elaborate tree from which presents were distributed and small coins given to the peasants.

In *War and Peace*, Leo Tolstoy tells of the visit of a group of Russians to the house of a count: "The mummers (some of the house serfs) dressed up as bears, Turks, innkeepers, and ladies—frightening and funny—bringing in with them the cold from outside and a feeling of gaiety, crowded, at first timidly, into the anteroom, then hiding behind one another they pushed into the ballroom where, shyly at first and then more and more merrily and heartily, they started singing, dancing and playing Christmas games."

Russian Christmas songs have long been known as *Kolyada*. The carols date back to pagan days and cover a variety of themes about gods and goddesses, but they were given Christian characteristics and so became the songs of Yuletide. A maiden dressed in white, representing the goddess of the sun, was drawn from house to house on a sled, attended by other maidens who sang carols.

The day after Christmas was a day for men to go visiting, and the women paid calls the following day. Foretelling the future at parties was a part of the holiday fun. Melted lead dropped in the snow could be interpreted by older women. The future could also be foreseen in an egg yolk dropped in a glass of water. An old custom—the five piles of grain—afforded more merriment. The younger women of the family made five piles of grain on the kitchen floor, each pile signifying something for the future, either wealth, poverty, marriage, death, or a life of single blessedness. At midnight a sleeping hen was taken from the roost and brought into the bright kitchen. While the hen was still asleep, its befuddlement caused great laughter, but as the hen awakened and sensed the grain it chose a pile, indicating the future of the girl involved.

The Russian child did not watch for Santa Claus to come down the chimney but stood by the windows to catch a glimpse of Babouschka hurrying by. Babouschka is a poor little crooked, wrinkled old woman who comes at Christmas time into everybody's house, peeps into every cradle, drops a tear, and goes away. She is always in a hurry as she goes about her search for the Christ Child. On Christmas Eve she pauses to give each little child a present.

Babouschka's story is similar to that of the Italian Befana, but is told with greater sadness. As she worked at her housecleaning, the Three Kings came by with their gifts for the Child. But she did not want to leave her cozy home and wished to finish her housework, so she refused to accompany the train of people following the star. Ever afterward she thought of the little Child, and one day she shut her house forever and set out on the long journey to find him. Little children know and love Babouschka as she comes softly, asking, "Is the young Child here?"

VELVET-COVERED BALLS

MATERIALS:

    styrofoam ball
    velvet
    ribbon, sequins, and braid for trim
    6" pipe cleaner

DIRECTIONS:

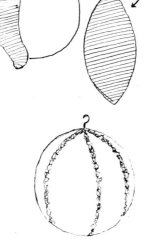

1. Cut six pieces of velvet on the bias (see pattern). A 5" ball needs a 7" length of velvet.
2. Starting from center of the ball and stretching to top and bottom, attach the velvet to the styrofoam ball with pins along edges of material. Overlap edges and continue applying pieces until ball is covered.
3. Insert 6" pipe cleaner firmly into top of ball for hanger.
4. Cover pinned seams with bands of trimming.
5. For a ball with petal design: cut twelve 3½" pieces of velvet, shaped as the large pattern. Starting from the hanger, center petals between seams of the velvet covering and pin to ball. Finish the petals with narrow braid trim. Repeat with six petals at bottom of ball.

DECORATED EGGSHELLS

MATERIALS:

egg
small figures; cutouts from Christmas cards
angel hair or cotton
soutache braid, rickrack, etc.
glitter

DIRECTIONS:

1. Buy extra-large white eggs. With cuticle scissors cut a small hole in side of egg—just enough to drain the egg.
2. Cut opening in side of the eggshell the desired size, about 1¼". Cut a small hole in top for an elastic thread hanger. Do this at once, after draining the egg, for the shell quickly becomes brittle. Wash out the inside of shell.
3. Glue angel hair or cotton inside the bottom of the shell to serve as a base for gluing tiny figures. These figures may be cut from Christmas cards, and background scenes may be added.
4. Around the opening glue soutache braid or tiny rickrack.
5. The outside of egg may be covered with glitter if desired. The inside may be colored for background.
6. Run a loop of elastic thread to inside of egg and knot so it will not slip through.

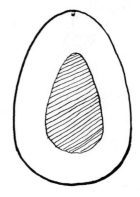

POLAND

The first star in the evening sky on Christmas Eve sets the theme for the celebration of the Polish Christmas as a Festival of the Star. With its appearance the day-long fast of *Wigilia* is ended, and families gather around the table to honor the Holy Child.

A small table before the family shrine holds Christmas candles and special pastries for the Christmas season. Sometimes the Nativity scene, assembled by young members of the family, is set in a box. Boys and girls like to carry it in processions and also to display it to their friends.

Market squares are fragrant with the scent of the evergreen woods as Christmas trees appear. Decorations made by schoolchildren are sold in shops to be used on the trees.

In homes straw on the floor and the table is a reminder of the stable where the Christ Child was born, and a chair is left vacant at the table for him. In some houses sheaves of wheat are used as decoration in the corners of the room, and these are later scattered in orchards for the birds.

Before the Christmas Eve meal is served, the master of the house or the oldest person present distributes the peace wafer. These are small white wafers which have been blessed by the church and are marked with scenes of the Nativity. Each member of the family shares his wafer with every other person at the table as a token of friendship and a symbol of peace on earth. The Christmas Eve supper consists of soup, fish of various kinds, cabbage, mushrooms, almonds, and sweetmeats made from honey and poppy seeds. Meat is never eaten at this meal. Token gifts may be placed at each plate.

After supper the Star Man arrives to examine the children in their religious knowledge. He may be the village priest or a friend in disguise.

The children are given small gifts which they believe are sent by the good Star of Heaven but carried to them by the Wise Men. The Wise Men are impersonated by three young men of the village known as Star Boys who carry an illuminated star and sing carols.

In rural areas the Star Boys are accompanied by groups of young people in disguise. Some dress as characters from the Nativity, but others may introduce animals or characters of folklore to add a note of amusement and entertainment. As they go from house to house singing carols, the performers receive treats. Songs and carols which celebrate the Polish Christmas are a combination of the religious and secular sentiments of the people and date back as far as the fifteenth century.

The midnight Mass on Christmas Eve is called *Pasterka*, the Mass of the Shepherds. Legend tells us that on this holy night the heavens open and those who have lived pure lives can see a vision of Jacob's ladder.

PEACOCK

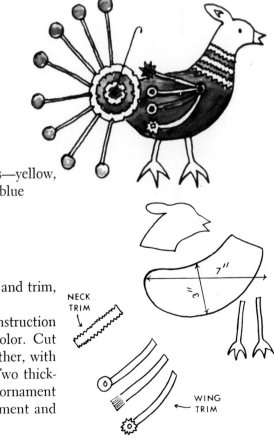

MATERIALS:

    construction paper in several colors—yellow,
       orange, white, red, light and dark blue
    6″ pipe cleaners
    wire

DIRECTIONS:

1. Make a pattern for body, head, feet, and trim, as shown in drawing.
2. Cut two bodies of one color of construction paper and two heads of another color. Cut four feet of yellow paper. Glue together, with the feet between the two bodies. (Two thicknesses of paper are necessary for an ornament of this size, giving body to the ornament and balancing the large tail.)

93

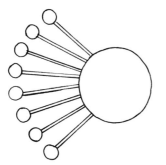

3. Cut a dot for eye of peacock and bands of two colors for decoration of the neck. Notch the bands on each side. Decorate the wing area with strips of colored paper and paste designs on the ends of the strips—circles or fringed paper.

4. Cut two circles 2½″ in diameter. Notch the edges shallowly. Paste on one circle four or five smaller notched circles of different colors, in graduated sizes.

5. Glue the two large circles together with eight pipe cleaners between, spreading the pipe cleaners out in a fan pattern. Glue the circle onto the body of the peacock at the tail. Glue ¾″ circles of gold paper at the outer end of each pipe cleaner.

6. Attach wire hanger through center of the larger circle at tail.

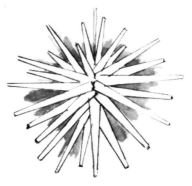

PORCUPINE

MATERIALS:

    white typing paper
    glitter
    2 white buttons
    white cord

DIRECTIONS:

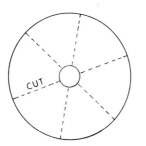

1. Cut twelve discs, 4″ in diameter, from typing paper. Draw a circle the size of a quarter in the center of each disc.

2. Divide each disc into six equal segments and cut from outer edge of circle to the edge of inner circle.

3. Roll each segment around a sharpened pencil to form a conical spike. Fasten with clear glue; slip the pencil out when glue is dry.

4. Place glitter in saucer. Scatter touches of glue

over the disc and roll in glitter while glue is wet.

5. Thread a large needle with white cord and tie a white button at end of cord. Run cord through the center of 12 discs and slip second button over the needle.

6. Squeeze the discs together and run the needle back through button, discs, and bottom button. Leave long cord for hanging.

ANGEL

MATERIALS:

    cardboard
    construction paper
    fancy paper

DIRECTIONS:

1. Make patterns, as illustrated.
2. Cut 2 bodies from cardboard.
   Cut dress and star of fancy paper, fringes of white paper.
3. Eyebrows are black, with red mouth and pink checks for face. These may be cut from paper.
4. Wings, crown, feet, and belt are of construction paper in harmonizing colors.
5. To assemble, paste wings, feet, and star to one cardboard body. Glue this to other angel body. Paste on the petticoat fringes top and bottom; then paste dress over these so fringed edges show.
6. Paste on belt, crown, and face.

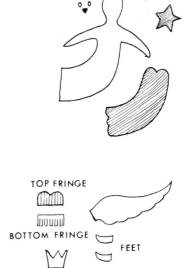

TOP FRINGE

BOTTOM FRINGE

FEET

FLAT PAPER CHAIN

MATERIALS:

colored paper

DIRECTIONS:

1. Make a pattern for circle 2¾" in diameter, with center cut out.
2. Fold paper and cut double circle on fold.
3. To make chain, loop one circle through another and continue looping each new circle through the preceding one. This is an easy decorative chain, requiring no paste.

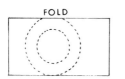

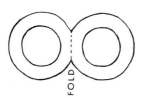

FISH

MATERIALS:

1½" styrofoam ball
construction paper of different colors
paint

DIRECTIONS:

1. Cut patterns for fish, as illustrated.
2. Roll a tube of construction paper 6½" long for body of fish, fitting one end around styrofoam ball. Glue edges together and pin to ball.
3. Cut tail fins of different colors, one slightly larger than other. Glue together and insert in tail of fish.
4. Use two colors for an accordion-fold fin on top of fish, two fins on lower body.
5. Form a cone for head (about 4" long), fitting large end over styrofoam ball and rolling to a point for the mouth. Pin to ball.
6. Decorate body with paint. Make a large round eye.

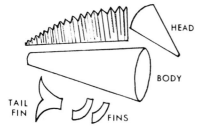

BIRDS

MATERIALS:

   construction paper in several colors
   small styrofoam ball
   gold spray paint

DIRECTIONS:

1. Cut two birds from construction paper.
2. Cut two pieces for wings, two pieces for smaller wings, and two black circles for eyes. Paste these on bodies of the birds so birds face each other.
3. Spray a styrofoam ball gold and pin a decorative star at top and bottom.
4. Cut two feet with pattern placed on fold. Paste fold to bird.
5. Fasten bird to ball by pinning feet to front and back of ball.

WINGS

FOLD

FEET

SHIELD

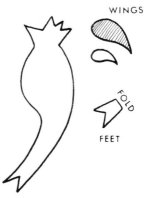

MATERIALS:

   heavy gold paper
   shiny red paper
   glitter, sequins

DIRECTIONS:

1. Cut the largest outline, A, of heavy gold paper.
2. Cut other pieces, B and C, of shiny red paper.
3. Paste B and C on A. Decorate with sequins and glitter. Cut edges of gold paper for fringed look.

TIDEWATER PLANTATION

Christmas had some early struggles in Colonial America. The Puritans of New England forbade its observance as a popish practice, and in Massachusetts fines were imposed on those who celebrated the day in any way, whether feasting or forbearing to work. It was in the South that Christmas customs and traditions were nurtured. In the Tidewater area the old customs of a light hearted English Christmas were practiced—with some additions and innovations which were to become tradition in the South.

The Tidewater—that part of the Atlantic coastal plain extending inward to the area reached by oceanic tides—became a region of large plantations and of the important commercial towns. In Tidewater Virginia, Christmas customs from England dominated the celebration of the season. The hanging of the greens, the Yule log, and the feasting reflected the mother country, and at the College of William and Mary at Williamsburg the students practiced the old custom of "barring out the teacher." Christmas began reverently with church services, after which the Virginian was free to entertain his friends and be entertained.

On the plantations the Tidewater aristocracy lived on a scale which astonished visitors. Hospitality was universal, and visitors came not for the day but for weeks. The Colonials liked parties, balls, and hunts, and the Christmas holidays combined them all. This season became a favorite time for weddings: George Washington and Martha Custis were married on Twelfth Night, 1759. Wedding guests came from far and near to White House, the plantation home of Martha Dandridge Custis on the Pamunkey River. From the kitchens came the dishes typical of the plantation Christmas for her wedding guests—hams, beef and pork, turkey and game, oysters, and rich fruit cakes.

William Byrd II of Westover wrote in his diaries of his own Christmas—devout attendance at church, followed by visits to friends during the holidays with much feasting and games. They enjoyed billiards, cards, skating on the ice, drinking wine, and being "merry with nonsense."

Virginia was rich in the greenery which Colonials used to decorate the house, and churches too were made festive with ivy, holly, and rosemary. A new custom arose in Virginia and other parts of the South which became tradition—the noise of firearms, expressed today in fireworks. Perhaps the custom rose as a salute from one neighbor to another across intervening acres. In the food department, oysters and oyster dressing were to become traditional—and if the wassail bowl was missing, the eggnog took its place.

In Williamsburg, Virginia, in 1842 there occurred an incident which gave Christmas a new turn and centered it upon the young members of the household. Here a young German, Charles Minnegerode, who taught at the College of William and Mary, asked permission of his friend Judge Nathaniel Beverly Tucker to set up a Christmas tree for the Tucker children, a tree such as his family would have in Germany. Judge Tucker agreed and planned a holiday party for the children.

The shining glass globes and tinseled ornaments of the German tree were lacking, but the young teacher and the children improvised, using strings of popcorn and gilded nuts. Globes of bright paper were substituted for glass balls. Many candles illuminated the tree, although holders were lacking and the candles had to be wired in place.

Children of friends were included in the first Christmas tree party. Neighbors and friends of the town asked to see the strange and beautiful creation for Christmas which had been so joyfully received by the children. Judge Tucker, until his death, continued to have a Christmas tree party for children. Each year the excitement was great as the children marched in, the youngest first, singing carols. Today, when restored Williamsburg re-enacts the Christmas of Colonial days with the blessing of the Yule log and other ceremonies, there stands a community Christmas tree near the Tucker house, reminding us that this handsome home was the one which gave to the area a new idea for Christmas.

CREWEL DECORATIONS

MATERIALS:

crewel linen and thread
felt

DIRECTIONS:

1. Using crewel thread, embroider a design on crewel linen—fruit, flowers, birds, butterflies, or animals. The finished ornament should be 3″ to 5″ in size, depending on shape and design.
2. The embroidered design may be finished in any of three ways.

   (a) Cut a linen piece the size of the work. With right sides together stitch on machine, leaving room for turning. Stuff with yarn or other material to ¼″ thickness. Close with blind stitching.

   (b) Cut the embroidered linen in a circle, allowing ½″ around the design plus the seam allowance. Sew to another circle of linen, turn and stuff thinly. Finish with yarn, overcast-stitching around edge of circle.

   (c) Cut around the design, leaving enough linen for seam. Glue design to a felt backing. This is the most difficult finish unless design is carefully chosen. Avoid design with points or angles.

FRUIT

MATERIALS:

salt
cornstarch
cake coloring
wire hooks
artificial leaves
wire

102

DIRECTIONS:

1. Mix together 2 cups salt and 2/3 cup water. Heat, stirring constantly.
2. Remove from heat and add to this a paste made from 1 cup cornstarch and ½ cup water colored with cake coloring. Stir together.
3. Mold into desired shapes. Place a hook in each ornament before it is dry. Wire artificial leaves to hook.
4. Rough edges may be smoothed with water while fruits are still moist.

Plums, figs, pears, apples, peaches, grapes, and lemons are effective on the Tidewater tree.

PAPER CUTOUT

MATERIALS:

construction paper

DIRECTIONS:

1. Trace around pattern for cutout on a folded piece of construction paper.
2. Cut out the design outline and the center spaces so that a lacy, openwork ornament results. Cut through both thicknesses of paper.
3. Unfold. Glue loop of thread at center for hanging.

Pattern adapted from *Christmas Make-It Ideas*, Volume X, p. 82.

TRIANGLE CUTOUTS

MATERIALS:

tissue paper
cardboard
white glue

DIRECTIONS:

1. Cut a supply of 2″ circles of tissue paper.
2. Cut from cardboard an equilateral triangle that fits the circle when centered on it. Cut a smaller equilateral triangle to use as a pattern for cutting out the centers of the circle.
3. Place the large cardboard pattern on the circle and draw around it. Trace the small triangle with a pencil and cut out.
4. Fold up the three scallop-shape edges of the circle which show around the large triangle. Crease well.
5. Glue the triangle cutouts together to form a ball. Leave the creased round edges free. Glue only on the folded edges, barely overlapping.
6. For a small ball, use ten circles. It is easier to assemble by gluing eight of the circles together in pairs, leaving two singles. Now glue two pairs together, then add a single to form rounded shape of half a ball. Assemble the others in same fashion, then glue the two halves together.
7. Attach loop for hanging with needle and thread.

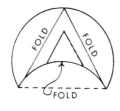

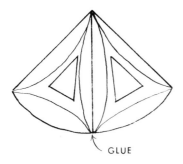

This ornament requires great accuracy in cutting and gluing.

TISSUE-CONE BALLS

MATERIALS:

tissue paper
white glue

DIRECTIONS:

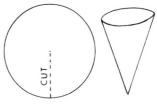

1. Cut a supply of tissue-paper circles in chosen color, 3″ in diameter.
2. Make a cone from each tissue circle by cutting it halfway through and overlapping edges until cone is formed. Glue in place.
3. Glue sides of cones together with points toward center to form a ball shape. Eighteen or twenty cones make a ball. Hang by thread.

ADDITIONAL ORNAMENTS

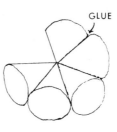

English walnuts, gilded and wired in clusters

Cranberries strung on dental floss

Popcorn strings

4″ x 6″ candy bags of Black Watch and Northern Scotch plaid

Crown for top of tree, fashioned from wire, covered with papier-mâché, and painted gold

MORAVIAN
TREE

The Moravian Church traces its origin to the movement for church reform led by John Hus, rector of the University of Prague and preacher in one of Prague's largest churches. Hus taught that the church of his day was no longer true to the New Testament gospel, a teaching which brought the condemnation of the church down upon him. He was burned at the stake in 1415. His followers formally organized under the name *Unitas Fratrum* (Unity of the Brethren) in 1457. Because much of its early history centered in Moravia, now a part of Czechoslovakia, the church later came to be known as the Moravian Church.

Persecution and the devastating effects of the Thirty Years War reduced the Brethren to a few scattered remnants in Central Europe. Then in 1722, under the leadership of Count Nikolaus von Zinzendorf, the church was revived in Germany. The Moravians launched a worldwide program of foreign missions which brought them to Georgia with Oglethorpe in 1735 to preach to the American Indians. The war with the Spanish threatened; their scruples against bearing arms forced them to abandon the Savannah property, and they went to Pennsylvania in 1740 and helped with the beginning of a settlement there. Count Zinzendorf himself chose the name of the central town of the Moravian settlement in Pennsylvania—Bethlehem, which was named on Christmas Eve, 1741.

In 1752 Bishop Spangenberg led a small group of Moravians to North Carolina to seek a tract of 100,000 unoccupied acres. He wrote that part of the trip from Norfolk was a "hard journey over very high, terrible mountains and cliffs. Part of the way we climbed on hands and knees." From two early settlements in the wilderness of

North Carolina, the Moravians branched out to found Salem as a trade and craft center. Here work on the town began in 1766; Salem was in full operation by 1772, with millwrights, gunsmiths, carpenters, and blacksmiths among the craftsmen.

Moravian settlements were marked by intensive religious life, missionary zeal, handicraft industries, education, and the cultivation of music. A girls' school was founded in 1772, which in 1802 became a boarding school, the second one in America. Moravian College (for men) was founded in 1807.

The church itself was an institution of great music. Most Moravian music was religious vocal music which called for instrumental accompaniment, especially an orchestra of violins. The Moravian orchestras were the earliest symphony orchestras in America. The first trombones in America were brought by the Moravians, and these instruments were used to announce all public, and some private, occasions.

There are a number of customs of the ancient church still in practice today in the Moravian churches. The best known are the Easter sunrise service and the love feast. The love feast was a part of the Christmas Eve observation at the founding of Bethlehem and at the first settlement in North Carolina. A Moravian love feast is a religious service in which Christian fellowship is emphasized. It is primarily a song service during which the congregation partakes of a simple meal—coffee and buns. Women of the church, dressed in white, quickly and quietly pass the baskets of soft buns, followed by men carrying mugs of coffee. Everyone in the congregation is served and all partake, participating in a ceremony of fellowship.

The Christmas Eve love feast is especially impressive and moving. In addition to the solemn sharing of food, there is a candlelight service. Every member of the congregation is given a lighted candle of beeswax, passed by the women dressed in white. The candles are held aloft as the bishop gives a blessing, and all hearts are rededicated to Christ, the Light of the World. A service for children is held on the afternoon of Christmas Eve, and there is another in the evening for adults.

The beeswax candles of the love feast are made by women of the Moravian Church who prepare the wax and mold the candles. Red-frilled holders or "petticoats" are wrapped around the bottom of the candle to prevent the dripping wax from burning the fingers.

The Moravian Christmas is distinguished by two forms of decoration—the star and the *putz*. The "Moravian star" itself has a history. It is not known who invented this star; apparently it originated in the evening handicraft sessions in Niesky, Germany, about 1850. In the 1880's Pieter Verbeek began to make the stars for sale. His son learned the art and later founded the Herrnhut star factory. For some years the two Verbeeks had charge of the bookstore in Herrnhut, and there they received orders for the stars which were shipped to many places, with directions for assembling them printed in four languages. The stars are made by an intricate process, with twenty-six sections, each three-sided. Formerly the stars held a lighted candle; today they are illuminated by electric bulbs. The star may be used at Advent, appearing on the first Sunday of Advent, or as a Christmas star, reserved until the evergreens are placed for Christmas.

The *putz* is an important part of the Moravian Christmas. The word *putz* comes from the German *putzen*, to adorn or decorate, and the *putz* is the Moravian form of the "Christmas yard" or "Christmas garden" with the Holy Family as the focal group. It is built under the Christmas tree and is a miniature landscape telling the story of Christ's birth. All sorts of additions or variations are allowed, and the *putz* may be tiny or take up a whole room.

Preparation begins early as the children go out to hills and woods to gather moss, rocks, roots, or tree stumps to be used as background. The father of the family builds a platform on which to assemble the scene; it is always low enough that the smallest child may easily look at the figures. The landscape of the *putz* may be woods, desert, or farmland, and whatever the fancy and imagination of the family desires may be included. Always the project is one of family participation, and a family *putz* grows larger and more beautiful with the years as new figures and sections are added. In the words of J. Kenneth Pfohl, pastor of Home Moravian Church, the *putz* tells the "old, old story which transformed the world and brought to home and childhood their greatest inspiration and blessing."

It is customary for Moravian families to go *putzing*—that is, visiting the homes of neighbors and friends to see the *putz*. The *putz* is seldom missing, even in childless homes. In Bethlehem, Pennsylvania, thousands of visitors view the *putz* at Central Moravian Church, and in Old Salem, North Carolina, thousands come to the Brothers House to see the moss-covered *putz* which takes up two rooms.

The *putz* at Old Salem is in two parts. The first is a reproduction of the town of Salem as it was during the period from 1830 to 1860, built to a scale of one inch to eight feet. The second and most important part is the Nativity scene which shows the town of Bethlehem and the surrounding country.

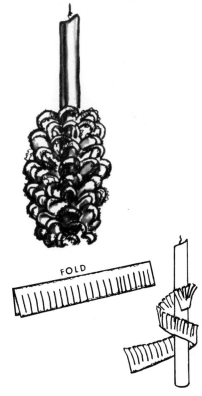

CANDLES AND "PETTICOATS"

MATERIALS:

natural beeswax candles (6″)
red crepe paper

DIRECTIONS:

1. Cut strips of red crepe paper 3½″ x 12″.
2. Fold each strip lengthwise and cut a fringe to within ½″ of the edge, cutting on folded edge.
3. Leaving the strip folded, wrap the lower half of a 6″ beeswax candle, starting in middle of candle and working down. Fasten ends with tiny straight pins.

MUSICAL INSTRUMENTS

MATERIALS:

3/16″ pine board
clear varnish
patterns of musical instruments

DIRECTIONS:

Patterns may be sketched from exhibit of instruments at Old Salem, North Carolina, or from articles and histories. If these are unavailable, sketches may be made of present-day instruments, as many musical instruments have changed little.

1. With jigsaw cut the instruments from 3/16″ pine.
2. Finish with clear varnish.
3. Strings may be added where needed for a realistic touch. Knot ends of threads and staple in place.

PINE CONES

MATERIALS:

pine cones
foil pan
red yarn

DIRECTIONS:

1. Bake pine cones in a 275° oven for a half hour. The sap will coat and brighten the cones. (Use a foil pan or line a baking pan with foil to catch the excess.)
2. Attach cones to tree with red yarn.

MORAVIAN STAR

MATERIALS:

unassembled 26-pointed star
paper clips

DIRECTIONS:

1. This intricate 26-pointed star of white paper may be purchased from a Moravian bookstore, unassembled.
2. The star is held together with paper clips. Even with instructions to follow, the star is a challenging bit of work.
3. The Moravian star did not hang on a tree but decorated hall or porch of the home.

APPLE RINGS

MATERIALS:

dried apple rings
red yarn

DIRECTIONS:

Tie the apple rings in clusters with red yarn.

SWEDEN

In Scandinavia there is a saying that Christmas lasts a whole month. Indeed, in Sweden the Yuletide season does extend from December 13, Saint Lucia Day, until January 13, Saint Knut's Day. Nowhere is Christmas celebrated more warmly than in this snowy land where custom, tradition, and folklore make the Yule time a festival of the home.

The Swedish Christmas is an old-fashioned one with all the ingredients of a picture-book Christmas—a perfect setting of glistening snow, hospitable tables, and Christmas trees with real candles and heirloom decorations. December is the darkest month of the year, with dusk descending in mid-afternoon. Preparations for Christmas become an antidote to darkness; many of the customs and practices belong to December alone and distinguish the season from days of everyday existence. Hospitality expands as everyone observes the old belief that the Christmas spirit must be kept in the house by offering each visitor a bite to eat.

Many practices of the Christmas season have ties with pagan belief. Even the thorough housecleaning has its story. In heathen times it was said that goblins, trolls, and other evil beings came into the house at this dark time of year and that they had power to bring disaster to the household and its people. Cleanliness could rout these evil beings, so every corner of the house, every drawer and cupboard, was made spotless. If the washing, scrubbing, and polishing give a holiday look to the house, one can enjoy it in today's Swedish home without believing in ghosts and goblins at all!

In the midst of the winter darkness comes the Lucia festival, when Sweden pays tribute on December 13 to Saint Lucia. Early in the morning the oldest daughter in the household rises before dawn to prepare coffee and buns, which she serves to other members of the family while they are still in bed. Lucia is clothed in a long, flowing white gown, and on her head she wears a wreath of greenery with seven lighted candles. Lucia's song as she moves from room to room is a Sicilian melody, "Santa Lucia." In Swedish it has many verses—new words set to an old melody—and the song promises that darkness will soon end:

> "Now shall another morn
> From rosy skies be born."

The first Lucia was not a Swedish girl, but was born in Sicily. On the eve of her marriage she gave all her dowry to the poor, an act so misunderstood that she was accused of witchcraft and burned at the stake on December 13, 304. Thereafter she was seen in many places where people needed help; once she appeared in a province of Sweden to feed the people during a period of famine. Lucia was canonized; her feast day, December 13, was the day of the winter solstice according to the unreformed calendar, and this day brings a message of hope, charity, and light to the Swedish people.

Originally Saint Lucia Day was observed as a family festival, but the celebration has become a community affair also. In cities and towns of Sweden today it is an occasion when hundreds of girls compete for the honor of being the year's outstanding Lucia. The tradition has continued in Swedish-American churches and organizations.

Preparation for Christmas begins in earnest after Saint Lucia Day. Housewives take great pride in the quality of food offered to guests and love to outdo each other in their Christmas baking. The Swedes say, "If we are going to have fattening Christmas food, it must be good," so this is the time of year when only the finest ingredients are used, no matter what the budget at other times. Many of the substantial and heavy foods reflect the agricultural roots of a people who lived mostly on farms until a hundred years ago. The older generation remembers a time when every family had its Christmas pig and no one would have dreamed of buying prepared food, even if there had been any available. Many women still prepare their food by inherited recipes, and limited kitchen space does not mean that the fragrant sausages and the great ham have disappeared from the Christmas menu.

Christmas Eve is the most important day of the season, and the climax of Christmas Eve centers around the Christmas tree. The tree came to Sweden from Germany in 1741 and immediately was adopted as a symbol of Christmas. The choosing of the tree is a matter of concern for every member of the family, and it is given a place of honor in the living room. Originally it was decorated rather sparingly, for the most part with lighted candles and perhaps silver paper and red apples. Many Swedes still keep strictly to wax candles with small red apples hung beneath for balance. It is still considered "most refined" not to overdecorate, but there are always cookies in many shapes and tassel candy (candy in colored papers with fringed ends). A new fashion is the use of colored glass balls.

Christmas Eve is a family day. At noon young and old gather in the kitchen for *doppa i grytan*, "dip-in-the-pot," a custom dear to the Swedish people. On the stove stands a large kettle with broth in which the ham, sausages, and other meats have simmered; on the table are slices of a special rye bread. Each person dips a piece of bread into the pot and eats it, a ceremony which serves as a reminder that once upon a time the only food was bread and broth and that every bit of food is precious. At the Christmas Eve luncheon one must remember not to eat too much because the dinner will be the richest and grandest meal of the year.

The Christmas Eve smorgasbord is as rich as the purse affords, and the Christmas ham must be a large one. Two dishes are traditionally served—*lutfisk* and rice pudding. The *lutfisk* is a sun-dried, lime-cured fish, and its pungent odor as it cooks means Christmas Eve. Before anyone may eat his pudding, he must make a rhyme. This rhyming with the rice affords much merriment, as does the maneuver to see that an unmarried person gets the single almond hidden in the pudding. The lucky almond means marriage by next Christmas.

After dinner the family gathers around the lighted tree for gifts which are brought by *Jul-Tomte*, a Santa Claus for Swedish children. The *Tomte* is a little gnome who lives on Swedish farms as guardian of the household. At Christmas a big bowl of rice porridge is set on the doorstep for him.

Christmas Day begins with early church service. In years past the service began as early as four o'clock, with church bells ringing their first call at two in the morning. In the dark morning lighted torches were carried or fastened to sleighs, and the approach to the church was very impressive through the snowy countryside. The Christmas music of the morning candlelit service is known and loved from earliest childhood:

> "All hail thou radiant morning-tide
> By holy tongues long prophesied."

Following Christmas Day, with its rest and relaxation, the season of hospitality gets in full swing. There is a great deal of visiting and many children's parties. One other celebration takes place, on January 6 (Epiphany), when the Star Boys go from house to house singing old hymns and folk songs. They wear long white robes and cone-shaped hats.

The Christmas season ends on January 13 as decreed by King Knut, who ruled the country from 1080 to 1086. Before Knut Day there are tree-plundering parties, a special event for children. The tree is lighted for the last time and singing, dancing, and games take place around it. At a signal, the children remove the ornaments from the tree. The cookies and candies are divided among them and a fruit drink is served with additional cake, for they are the honored guests. The tree, stripped of its decoration, is carried out with the song,

> "After twenty days on Knut
> We dance the Christmas tree out."

STAR

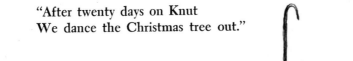

MATERIALS:

heavy white paper
gold paint
wire

DIRECTIONS:

1. Cut 16 pieces of A, using heavy white paper. Paint a thin line of gold along edges.
2. Crease on dotted lines. Bring sides of paper in toward center. This forms a cone shape with 3 points. Glue together.

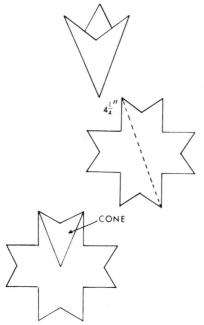

3. From heavy white paper cut an 8-pointed star 4¼″ from a point to opposite point. Gild edges on both sides.
4. Glue 8 cones to each side of star. Place a cone on the star with seam side down and with points of star and points of cone together. (A cone will cover half of two points, not one whole point.)
5. Add touches of gold paint on the center creases of star and attach a wire for hanging.

ELF

MATERIALS:

piece of lightweight wood, about 2″ x 2″ x 6½″
paint—red, green, royal blue, and skin tone
small hook and wire

DIRECTIONS:

1. On a lathe shape the wood to a cylinder 1½″ in diameter and 6½″ in length. Sand until smooth.
2. Beginning about 2¾″ from one end, taper wood to a conical shape.
3. Paint a red cap 2½″ down from top point.
4. Paint a green band ¼″ wide below the red cap.
6. Use skin-tone paint for a face; make eyes white with a black dot; paint a long white beard in shape of an apron.
7. Paint the rest of cylinder royal blue.
8. Fasten hook and wire hanger at tip of cap on the back side.

SNOWBALLS

May be purchased from Shopping International.

MR. AND MRS. CLAUS

MATERIALS:

lightweight wood
paint in red, royal blue, green, yellow, and
    white
yarn, gray and white

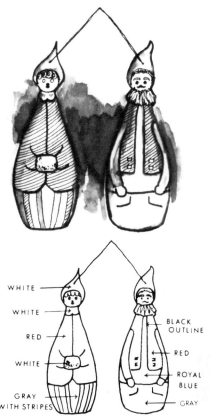

DIRECTIONS:

1. On a lathe turn two figures shaped as illustrated. Figures are 3½″ tall, 1½″ in diameter at bottom and 2½″ at center.
2. Paint as shown in sketches.
3. Glue gray yarn curls on Mrs. Claus and a gray beard on Mr. Claus.
4. Crochet caps and attach to head with glue.
5. Place small nail in top of each head. Wrap ends of 6″ wire around nails and hang as one ornament.

WHITE
WHITE
RED
WHITE
GRAY
WITH STRIPES

BLACK
OUTLINE
RED
ROYAL
BLUE
GRAY

PAPER BIRDS

MATERIALS:

lightweight colored paper, craft tissue or gift-
    wrap paper
cardboard
glitter

DIRECTIONS:

1. Cut two rectangles of colored paper, one 13″ x 9″ for wings, the other 11″ x 7″ for the tail.
2. Fold the rectangles lengthwise, accordion-style, making ⅜″ pleats. While paper is folded, notch each side of the paper so that the strip looks like rickrack. Trim end at an angle.

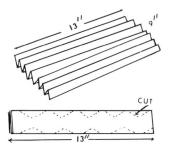

13″
9″
CUT
13″

121

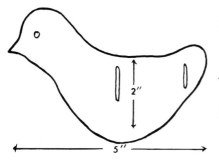

3. Cut a cardboard body for bird and cover each side with the lightweight paper. Make a slot for wings and another for tail.
4. Insert the folded papers in proper slots and spread out the pleats.
5. Glue a circle of glitter for eye.

TASSEL CANDY

MATERIALS:

colored tissue paper or cellophane
gold cord
small cylinder-shaped candy

DIRECTIONS:

1. Cut pieces of paper 7" x 5".
2. Roll paper lengthwise with piece of candy in center. Glue edge or fasten with gummed seal.
3. Fringe both ends of paper 1½".
4. Use a 10" length of gold cord for tying, wrapping the cord around each end and leaving the center for hanging.

FISHING CORK BIRDS

MATERIALS:

2" fishing cork ball
1" fishing cork ball
9 round toothpicks
tempera paints
1 screw eye
wire

DIRECTIONS:

1. Glue the two cork balls together, using the smaller one for head. Paint with tempera

(bright blue, red, yellow, or black). Paint eyes and wings in contrasting colors.

2. Center a full-length toothpick in the middle of the large cork (just back of the head) for the tail. Add six other toothpicks in a line, each pick shorter than the one before.
3. Make a beak using two toothpicks and leaving the pointed ends on the outside.
4. Place a small screw eye in the head or center of the back and run a thin wire through this for hanging.

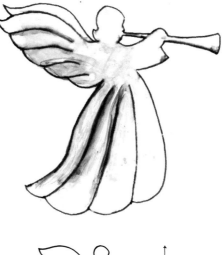

FOIL ANGEL

MATERIALS:

heavy gold decorator foil 9″ x 10″

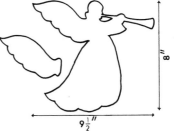

DIRECTIONS:

1. Cut the two pieces of the pattern from foil.
2. Mark inside design lines with a pointed tool such as a DRY ball-point pen.
3. Staple wing to body.

WOODEN ANGEL

MATERIALS:

wooden clothespin or wood turned on lathe
gold or silver paper
gold or silver braid
paint—yellow, sky blue, pink, black, and skin-tone
nail
foil paper

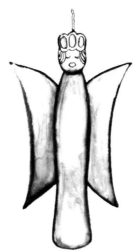

DIRECTIONS:

1. Paint wooden clothespin a light color—golden yellow or sky blue. With skin-tone

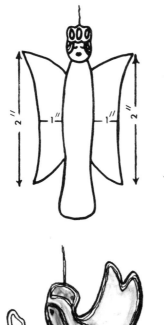

paint sketch a face, with black lines for eyes and pink for mouth and cheeks. Make yellow hair.

2. Make a crown of gold or silver braid. A ½″ braid with loop at edge makes a nice crown.
3. Cut wings of foil paper, 2″ from tip to tip and wide enough to extend 1″ on each side of body. Attach to center back ½″ below neck.
4. Hang by small wire attached to nail in top of head.

COOKIES

Decorate the Swedish tree further with cookies in the shape of hearts and angels. Ice the cookies white and edge the heart with a pink trim. Outline the angel with clear yellow. Use gold cords for hanging.

Authentic Swedish recipes for Christmas cookies may be used. However, because of the fragility of edible cookies, it is better to use a recipe for decorative lasting cookies (see Finland).

WOVEN NUT BASKETS

MATERIALS:

4 pieces of reed 5½″ long
1 piece of reed, full length cut
1 piece 12″ reed for handle

DIRECTIONS:

1. Soak reeds three hours in tap water.
2. Locate the center of the four reeds and form a cross.

3. Using long reed, bind the four reeds with three wraps.
4. Now separate the reeds so they appear as the spokes of a wheel. Weave over and under the spokes with the long reed, or weaver. Do not pull the weaver to tighten, just weave closely. If basket dries out during weaving, dip into tap water and resume weaving.
5. Insert the 12″ reed into basket on opposite sides to make handle, and strengthen it with glue.
6. Fill the basket with filberts and other nuts.

YARN DOLL

MATERIALS:

Medium to heavy weight yarn

DIRECTIONS:

1. Cut thirty to forty 18″ lengths of yarn, depending on weight of yarn.
2. Group these together lengthwise, tie tightly at center, and fold.
3. Tie again tightly 1½″ from first tying. This forms the head.
4. On each side part off enough threads to form the arms. Tie tightly at wrist location.
5. Tie loosely at waist.
6. Part the remaining threads into two equal parts to form legs, and tie tightly at ankle location.
7. Using contrasting color, tie knots around two or three threads at eye, nose, and mouth location to form facial features.
8. A ribbon bow may be added around the neck or atop the head for decoration.

TREE OF JESSE

The Christmas tree, glowing with light and topped by a shining star or an angel, symbolizes Christ as the Light of the World and brings the true message of Christmas. The Tree of Jesse, with its symbols representing Old Testament stories and events leading up to the birth of Christ, is another approach to the meaning of Christmas.

The representation of the Tree of Jesse is based upon the prophecy of Isaiah 11:1-2: "And there shall come forth a rod out of the stem of Jesse, and a branch shall grow out of his roots: and the spirit of the Lord shall rest upon him." In works of art the genealogy of Christ is frequently shown in the form of a tree which springs from Jesse, the father of David, and bears as its fruit the various ancestors of Christ.

The Jesse Tree symbols transform a Christmas tree into a "family tree" of Christ, since each ornament is a symbol of an ancestor or of a prophecy which foretells his coming. The symbols are the sun, the tablets of the Law, the key of David, Bethlehem, the root of Jesse, Noah's ark, the Ark of the Covenant, the altar of holocaust, the apple, the Paschal Lamb, the pillar of fire, manna, the star of David, Jacob's ladder, Jonah in the whale, the Temple, the crown and the scepter, the sword of Judith, the burning bush.

The sun represents Christ as bringing eternal life and light, and is based on the prophecy of Malachi: "But unto you that fear my name shall the Sun of righteousness arise with healing in his wings." The six-pointed Star of David symbolizes the lineage of Christ from the royal house of David. The burning bush symbolizes the Virgin Birth, and the prophecy of the birth is seen in the Bethlehem-emblem. The apple is a symbol of Christ, who took upon himself the burden of man's sin, and Jacob's ladder is interpreted as Christ reuniting mankind to God. The ladder has also been interpreted in a moral sense, with each of the fifteen rungs standing for a specific virtue. The lamb is one of the favorite, and most frequently used, symbols of Christ in all periods of Christian art. A typical reference is John 1:29, "The next day John seeth Jesus coming unto him, and saith, Behold the Lamb of God, which taketh away the sin of the world." Noah's ark is a symbol of baptism, and Jonah in the whale symbolizes death and resurrection.

The stories of the Old Testament have been an unlimited source of inspiration for the visual arts. The burning bush was the subject of the triptych painted by Nicolas Froment in the thirteenth century. The star of David was a popular symbol in stained glass windows, as at the Cathedral of Lyons.

The Jesse Tree was an early form of design for the stained glass windows of great cathedrals, such as Chartres. In the portrayal of the descent of Christ from the line of David, there may be as few as four or five figures or as many as fifty. The twisting branches of the tree always start with Jesse and end at the top with Christ. The Tree of Jesse window in the cathedral at Chartres is full of meaning and symbolism. In the lowest panel Jesse is lying upon a couch; from his loins rises the stem of a tree which branches out into scrolls enclosing seated figures of the sons of Jesse holding the branches. Next to the upper panel is the Virgin; the upper panel holds the figure of Christ, much larger, with the dove descending from above. On either side of the panels in semicircular spaces are the prophets who foretell the coming of Christ. A border of interlacing lines and flowers resembling those in the center panel completes the design of this famous window.

At Sens Cathedral the Jesse window is a little different, for it shows not only the ancestors of Christ; a donkey on one of the branches honors the animal that played so great a part in the life of Jesus.

JESSE TREE

MATERIALS:

½" plywood
green styrofoam, 2" thick
wire
artificial boxwood
7 electric candles

DIRECTIONS:

1. The seven-branched Jesse Tree is cut from ½" plywood. A frame of green styrofoam, cut in the same pattern, is wired to the wooden tree and covered with artificial boxwood of fine quality.
2. A small electric candle is attached to the tip of each branch.

TREE EMBLEMS

MATERIALS:

1 set of patterns for emblems
white mat board
gold paint
wire or nylon thread

DIRECTIONS:

1. Patterns for the 19 emblems may be purchased from Liturgical Press, Collegeville, Minnesota, with instructions for making.
2. Cut patterns from white mat board, using craftsman's knife or razor blade. Cuticle scissors aid in exactness. Use only white mat board (gold has white edges when cut).

3. Use best quality gold paint. All ornaments are gold and white.
4. Hang ornaments by thin wire or nylon thread.
5. Make Star of David of two layers of drawing board with ½" of styrofoam between.

UKRAINE

Today the Ukraine is one of the constituent republics of the Soviet Union. The history of the country is one of turbulence, for the Ukraine is, as the name signifies in Russian, a borderland. During the fourteenth century it was dominated by Lithuania and by Poland. In 1667 Poland was obliged to cede the northeast Ukraine to Russia, and more of the country was given to Russia during the eighteenth century by the Partition of Poland.

In the days when Christmas was more generally observed, it began with a forty-day fast, during which no meat was served, and ended with the appearance of the first star on Christmas Eve. All day long before Christmas it was the custom among native Ukrainians to fast until the evening meal; even the children were faithful to this tradition. Before the meal, as the table was prepared, Ukrainian mountaineers observed certain superstitious rituals which were centuries old. These included tying string around the legs of the table with a wish that the fruit trees would not break in the wind and laying a small ax head under the table with the wish that tools would be saved from rust and breakage. Hay was spread under the table and placed under the beautifully embroidered cloth as a symbol of the lowly place where the Christ Child first lay and to show the humility of the family.

A great sheaf of wheat was saved from the summer harvest for Christmas Eve, when it was placed in the corner of the room under an ikon and decorated with ribbons, flowers, and a small wreath of basil. It was considered only proper to do this since wheat was the chief product of the farm—indeed, of the whole country.

When the excited children called that the star was in the sky, the father of the household appeared with a large braided loaf of bread—the Christmas bread—in which there was a lighted candle. Followed by the children, he circled the house three times, saying prayers for his family and dear ones and for the beasts of the barnyard. Previously the cattle had been given an extra portion of fodder so that they might be content on the night of the miracle.

The Christmas Eve dinner was a twelve-course meal, each course commemorating one of the twelve Apostles. After dinner carolers visited the house to sing the traditional songs of Christmas, *Kolyada*.

Christmas was a three-day holiday devoted to church and visiting. The priest might also visit to bless the house and examine the children in their catechism.

Preparation for Christmas included a special housecleaning and often a nice clean coat of whitewash. Outside, the father cleaned courtyard and barnyard so that everything would be in order. Quantities of wood were cut and hauled to last through the holiday, for it was not considered proper to cut wood during the Nativity celebration. Inside the house newly embroidered towels were hung out, and every speck of dust routed. It was considered good luck, however, to find a spider web in the house on Christmas. The story goes that once a poor woman was unable to provide trimmings for her children's Christmas tree. When she woke on Christmas morning, she found that the first light of the sun struck the cobwebs and turned them to silver. Her tree was decorated—the spider and his web had brought good luck.

QUEEN ANNE'S LACE

MATERIALS:

    fresh-cut flowers of Queen Anne's lace
    large shallow box
    sand
    white paint and silver glitter

DIRECTIONS:

1. Cut stems of flowers short and spread face down on a thin layer of sand on bottom of the box.
2. Gently sift sand over flowers until completely covered.

3. Leave until dry (about two weeks) then lift out and shake off sand.
4. Spray with white paint and sprinkle with silver glitter immediately, before paint dries.

SPIDERS

MATERIALS:

Creepy-crawler molds
Plastigoop
glitter
papier-mâché

DIRECTIONS:

1. Make three sizes of Plastigoop spiders. Make large spider for top of tree of papier-mâché. Cover spiders heavily with silver glitter.

GLASS BALLS

MATERIALS:

2½" glass Christmas balls
bleach

DIRECTIONS:

Soak the balls in pure bleach to remove color and leave clear glass.

SNOWFLAKES

Directions for crocheting snowflakes may be found in *Christmas Helps, 1966* (see Resources). Starch so they will hang gracefully on tree.

SPIDER WEB

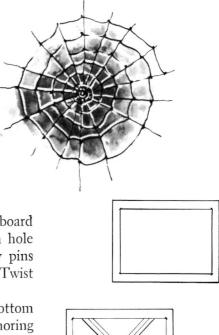

MATERIALS:

poster board, 22" x 28"
3 bobby pins
supply of hair wire
silver glitter

DIRECTIONS:

1. Punch hole in each corner of poster board about 2" from edges. Stretch wire from hole to hole around the board, using bobby pins to anchor it on the back of the board. Twist ends together at last hole.
2. Run 3 wires from the top wire to the bottom wire diagonally from left to right, anchoring ends of each wire to the original wire by twisting it several times.
3. Run 3 wires from top to bottom diagonally from right to left.
4. Turn the board and do the same thing from side to side.
5. Take a piece of wire 12" long and gather all diagonal wires together in the center. With excess wire go around and around the center, over and under the wires, until a circle about the size of a quarter is formed. Now start picking up each wire in rotation, going over and under, then back over the same wire. Press the wire hard against the board with a finger and pull sharply with the other hand; pick up the next wire and repeat until web is complete. As one piece of wire is exhausted, anchor it to the closest diagonal wire and begin with the next length at the same place.
6. Remove from board, spray with glue, and dip in silver glitter. Repeat if not glittered enough.

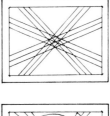

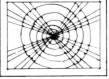

FINLAND

Finland begins the long season of Christmas celebrations on the last Sunday in November, which is called "Little Christmas." At this time majestic trees are erected in the marketplaces of cities, and forests of Christmas trees, great and small, are for sale. Villages and stores add holiday decorations. In the home Little Christmas is a day for parties, with songs, gingerbread snaps, and the first sampling of the Christmas pudding. Many of the traditional ornaments are made on Little Christmas.

An old custom still practiced in parts of Finland is the plaiting of a canopy of straw to be suspended from the ceiling. Paper stars hung from this straw "ceiling" reflect the light of the lamps and the fire below, suggesting a starlit sky to the children. Formerly straw was spread on the floor of the farmhouse to suggest the manger, and all the family enjoyed it as a center of Christmas games.

On Christmas Eve, with all preparations complete for the holiday, there is a visit to the sauna, a custom centuries old. The traditional bath house or sauna is a separate building where stones are heated until red hot; then cold water is poured over them to produce steam which relaxes and cleanses the bather. No Finn is too poor or too busy or too lazy to prepare the fire and carry the water for a sauna. The Finnish passion for cleanliness is a national trait.

After the sauna, everyone puts on his finery in readiness for the festivities. The family gathers for a meal of porridge, fish, and other dishes. Following supper, the big moment for the children is the arrival of Santa Claus, who comes early in the evening from far-away Lapland. Everyone retires early, for Christmas church services start at seven. In the days of sleighs each family attached as many bells as possible to the sleigh, so that the drive to church was a joyous and merry part of the holiday celebration.

Christmas Day in Finland is a quiet family day, with a dinner which includes roast suckling pig and the traditional rice pudding with one almond for good luck in the coming year. Like their Swedish neighbors, the Finns have a taste for ham, but they may bake theirs in a rye-dough crust and serve with it their own turnip pudding instead of the Swedish accompaniment of red cabbage.

On December 26, Saint Stephen's Day, there are traditional Saint Stephen's races when horses are raced along snowy country roads. This is a day too for visiting relatives and friends, and the evening is usually spent in dancing. The friendly hospitality of the Finns is charmingly expressed in their national epic, the *Kalevala:*

> "Benches will not sing unto us,
> Save when people sit upon them,
> Nor will floors hold cheerful converse
> Save when people walk upon them,
> Neither are the windows joyful
> If the lords should gaze not from them,
> Nor resound the table's edges,
> If men sit not round the tables."

FINNISH HEAVEN

MATERIALS:

8' x 10' frame made of 1 x 4's
10 8' lengths of ¾" rope
8 10' lengths of ¾" rope
large staples
2 bales of straw
sea oats
masking tape
heavy-duty thread

DIRECTIONS:

1. Make a frame of 1 x 4's.
2. Attach rope to frame with large staples.

Weave the rope, one over, one under, making squares fairly uniform.

3. Soak the straw in water overnight. Tie straw and sea oats in small bundles; put three bundles together with masking tape. Fireproof.

4. Hang the bundles at intersections of the rope and fill in with loose straw.

FINNISH HEAVEN ORNAMENTS

MATERIALS:

silver poster paper and lighter weight paper
colored cellophane

DIRECTIONS:

1. From a few basic star patterns make different designs of varying sizes. Hang 8 to 10 dozen stars on an 8' x 10' "heaven."

2. Examples of design. Cut 2 six-pointed stars of silver poster paper. At center cut out a design of 8 diamond shapes. Paste the two stars together with red cellophane between.

    Cut 2 six-pointed stars of 6" size. Cut a 1¾" circle from the center of each. In one of the stars make two ½" cuts opposite each other from edge of circle toward point of star. Slip the other star into the cuts so that the stars are at right angles. Hang a 1" star in the circle.

3. Hang all the stars in the "heaven" by thin nylon thread, varying the lengths.

TREETOP STAR

MATERIALS:

   3 pieces of reed 8" long
   white yarn
   silver paper

DIRECTIONS:

1. Fasten 3 reeds together at center, as shown. Tie with nylon thread or glue securely. Cut 2 six-pointed stars (2¾") from silver paper. Place one under and one on top of reeds at the center and glue together.
2. Make four small notches in each reed to hold the yarn, starting ¼" from end and spacing them ¼" apart.
3. Start with the inside row of yarn. Go from A to B, loop around reed at notch (use glue for greater strength); go to C and loop around reed at notch; return to A. Make 4 rows.
4. Make another triangle by running yarn in the same way from D to E to F and back to D to complete a six-pointed star.

SUNBURST

MATERIALS:

   20 pieces of reed, 3" and 4" in length
   modeling clay
   legal seals, 1" and 1½"
   silver spray or paint
   thread

DIRECTIONS:

1. Dip reeds in water and lay in rows to dry straight.

2. Flatten a marble-sized piece of clay to a size smaller than the seal to be used.
3. Arrange dried, straightened reed in a radiating sunburst pattern, anchoring it in the clay. Place four long pieces in the shape of a cross and fill in with shorter pieces.
4. Put glue on clay center to secure reeds in place. Dry, then cover the center with seals, painted silver. Glue in a long loop of thread under the seal for hanging.
5. Design may be made smaller, or may be shaped, when finished by clipping with sharp shears.

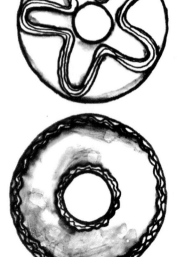

COOKIES

MATERIALS:

cookies
decorating icing in red and blue

DIRECTIONS:

1. Make cookies from following recipe for long-lasting cookies, which are for *decoration only*. Cut the dough in 3″ circles, some solid and some doughnut shaped.
2. Decorate heavily with red and blue icing, using a variety of designs.

COOKIE DOUGH

INGREDIENTS:

4 cups all-purpose flour
½ teaspoon salt
¾ cup soft butter
1½ cups sugar

2 eggs
½ teaspoon vanilla
Almond extract

DIRECTIONS:

1. Sift flour with salt. In large mixer bowl beat the sugar and butter until light and fluffy, using medium speed. Add eggs one at a time, beating well. Add the flavoring. Beat in the flour, a small amount at a time, using low speed. Beat until smooth.
2. Roll dough to ⅛" thickness and cut out cookies. If the dough seems too soft, refrigerate till firm.
3. Bake for 10 to 15 minutes in a 350° oven. Cool on wire rack and ice when cool. This is a hard cookie with the appearance of a fine sugar cookie. Will last for years.

COOKIE ICING

INGREDIENTS:

2 pounds confectioner's sugar
¾ cup egg whites
1 teaspoon cream of tartar

DIRECTIONS:

1. In a large bowl combine the ingredients at low speed of mixer. Beat until blended.
2. At high speed beat 5 minutes or until icing stands in stiff peaks.
3. Color with red and blue cake coloring.
4. If icing is too thin, add sugar.

This makes a large amount of icing. What is left may be stored in refrigerator or frozen. Commercial icing in aerosol can may be used if desired.

UNITED STATES COMMUNITY TREE

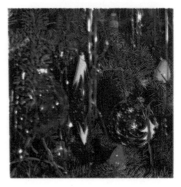

Christmas in the United States is the most exciting holiday of the year. The sparkle of lights and gay decorations, the shopping and the baking, parties and family gatherings, the carol singing and Nativity scenes, charity projects and church services—all blend joyfully to create a holiday of reverence and gaiety.

Customs and traditions of many nations are interwoven in the American Christmas. From Germany we received our Christmas tree, from Austria the beautiful carol "Silent Night," and Saint Nicholas came to us by way of Holland. Like English children, American tots hang their stockings by the fireplace.

But distinctly American is Santa, the joyous symbol of gift-giving at Christmas. The name developed from *Sinter Klass*, the name Dutch settlers in New York called Saint Nicholas. American children loved the kindly *Sinter Klass* but called him Santa Claus.

The sleigh and reindeer were introduced as Santa's mode of transportation in 1823 in a poem written by Clement C. Moore, an American poet and educator, for his children. The poem was, of course, "A Visit from Saint Nicholas," later known as "The Night Before Christmas." Gradually the kindly saint in bishop's robe and miter became a "right jolly old elf" who was dressed all in fur from his head to his toes. In 1863 when Thomas Nast, a widely known cartoonist, drew a picture of Santa, the transformation was complete.

Today in America the community tree lends a special kind of observance to the Christmas season. An event for all the nation is the lighting of a Christmas tree by the President of the United States. In 1923 Calvin Coolidge lighted the beautiful tree which had been cut in his native Vermont and shipped to Washington as a gift for the

President from Middleburg College, Vermont. This ceremony established the custom of an annual national Christmas tree-lighting ceremony by following Presidents.

Across the country there is hardly a town or city which does not have its own community tree. In 1909 the city of Pasadena, California, decorated an outdoor tree with electric lights to begin a practice which has become custom throughout the nation. New York set up its "tree of lights" in 1912, and the next year Philadelphia followed with a children's Christmas tree at Independence Square. Today there is wide variety among community trees, some cities claiming the tallest or the largest living Christmas tree, or choosing a setting which gives the community a special significance.

An impressive Christmas ceremony which is held annually in our country's out-of-doors is the carol service at King's Canyon National Park, California. In the part of the park known as the General Grant Grove there are giant sequoia trees which are without doubt the oldest living things in the world. Some trees were stately giants when the star led the Wise Men to the cradle of the Christ Child. Thus it seems peculiarly fitting that these giants of the forest should form the setting for a solemn celebration of the birth of Christ.

In 1925 a group of citizens from nearby Sanger held a Christmas ceremony at the foot of the largest and most famous tree in the park. This tree measures 40 feet thick at the base and towers upward almost 275 feet. It was named in 1867 in honor of General Grant, and in 1926 was officially dedicated as the Nation's Christmas Tree. The Yuletide services at the foot of the tree are always held at high noon on Christmas Day.

The community tree had a different meaning in the early part of the century, and there are many Americans who remember the time when one big Christmas tree served the whole town. This was set up in town hall, church, or schoolhouse. Around it centered a Christmas entertainment or program which included recitations and songs, perhaps a play or speech. In some areas the gifts of parents and friends were presented to children at the Christmas tree; in others all children were given bags of candy and nuts or poor children were especially remembered.

BRAZIL

Brazil is a vast country, and the word to sum up this amazing land is "diversity." A guidebook of recent date has said that a tourist coming to Brazil will find everything he expected and lots more he never dreamed existed. The country is so big and covers so many square miles that nothing is "typically" Brazilian. The people are a mixture of Portuguese settlers, Indian natives, and imported Africans. To this has been added peoples from Italy, Germany, Poland, England, and Japan.

Brazil was discovered by the Portuguese in 1500, and with the conquerors and planters came the Roman Catholic Church. In addition to the many customs brought over from Portugal, the Christmas festivals have gathered many features and traditions of each locality. These have given the season a particular charm and enrichment, with quaint ceremonies, folk songs, and dances.

Christmas comes in mid-summer instead of mid-winter in Brazil, so it is a time for picnics, boating excursions, fireworks, and festivals. Most of the great cities of Brazil are coastal, and going to the beach is part of the holiday celebration. As a resident of Rio de Janeiro said, "Christmas just isn't Christmas if I can't spend it with my family on the beach."

On Christmas Eve open-air dancing and carols occupy the time leading up to the Christmas Eve supper and midnight mass. Religious and civic groups celebrate the open-air festivals with the distribution of gifts to underprivileged children. These affairs are attended by many people of all classes in an atmosphere of music, flags, and flowers. Protestant missionaries have introduced the "white gift" Christmas. Though many of the people are poor, they know of others in greater need and bring their white-wrapped gifts to the church to help make a dinner for the very poor.

In the home the manger scene is set up early in December. Each day the figures of the Three Kings are moved forward a little, and on Christmas Eve the Christ Child is placed in his crib. The tree is seen first on Christmas Eve, and around it the whole family sings carols. Gifts are given on Christmas Eve, but the Day of the Three Kings vies with Christmas in the distribution of gifts, especially to children, who set out their shoes for the presents which symbolize the visit of the Wise Men to the Christ Child.

Foreign influence has brought jolly Santa Claus and all that we associate with him to Brazil. Santa Claus (*Sao Nicolau* or *Papa Noël*) jogs socially along with the old traditions, even though there isn't a chimney for him to descend. A mild movement some years ago to depose Santa in favor of Grandpapa Indian failed to banish old Santa and his Christmas paraphernalia.

The Christmas tree in Brazil today often is decorated with the same ornaments found on trees in the United States. In this tropical area it is usually of imitation pine. In earlier years the Christmas tree was an attempt to create the evergreen tree seen on Christmas cards and in the illustrated magazines which came into the country through increasing international communication. A native tree, stripped of its foliage, was covered with paper. Often strips of paper dangled from branches to simulate the graceful swag of pine and spruce trees. Cotton was used on the tree for snow.

TROPICAL BIRDS

MATERIALS:

cardboard
cotton
crepe paper
acrylic polymer emulsion, tube each of orange, yellow, black
long and short colored feathers
wire

DIRECTIONS:

1. Cut body of bird from cardboard. It should be about 6″ long from beginning of beak to beginning of tail feathers. Spread paste over cardboard body.
2. Cover body with several thicknesses of cotton. Use more cotton in middle of the bird to make a rounded body.
3. Cut white crepe paper into 2″ strips. Cover one side with wallpaper paste and wrap strips around cotton bird. Dry thoroughly.
4. Paint body of bird with yellow and orange polymer. Paint the beak yellow, and paint a large black eye. Finish both sides.
5. Attach a tail of long colored feathers; use short feathers for wings.
6. Bend wire to make feet; stick these into the cotton body.

FOIL TASSEL

MATERIALS:

> foil icicles
> aluminum foil
> wire

DIRECTIONS:

1. Fold about fifty icicles to make a 4″ tassel. Wire at center, leaving an inch of wire for hanger.
2. Cut a 2″ circle of heavy aluminum foil. Cut to center of circle at one point and make a cone by stapling cut edges together. Slip this cone over the wire at the top of the icicles.

PAPER FLOWERS

MATERIALS:

   tissue paper
   florist's wire, green floral tape
   glitter

DIRECTIONS:

1. Cut flowers from tissue paper in colors you desire.
2. Place petals together in numerical order, with No. 1 the base of flower. (For a fuller flower, use two or three of each number.)
3. Run a florist's wire from the under side up through the center, then back to under side, and fasten by twisting. Cover the wire with green floral tape.
4. Decorate edges of petals with glitter as desired.

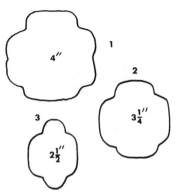

STARS

MATERIALS:

   cardboard
   aluminum foil
   glitter
   nylon cord

DIRECTIONS:

1. Cut 2" or 3" stars from cardboard.
2. Cover both sides with aluminum foil.
3. Glitter heavily.
4. Hang by nylon cord or thread.

MEXICO

In Mexico the Christmas season is a time when festive social life is happily blended with the religious observance of Christ's birth. The gay holiday begins on December 16 and ends on January 6 with the observance of Epiphany.

Early in December the colorful Christmas markets offer all the gifts and accessories necessary for the celebration of the great day. Baskets, toys, dolls, figures of the Holy Family, and colorful flowers are for sale. Assorted cakes, cheeses, and fruits appear in booths. Indians from small villages in the mountains bring their wares of leather, reed, clay, and wood. And everywhere are the bright piñatas needed for the *posadas.*

Posada means inn or lodging house, and this is the name given in Mexico to the ceremony which commemorates the trials and hardships of Mary and Joseph in their attempt to find shelter in Bethlehem. For nine evenings the procession takes place, ending on Christmas Eve.

The house must be decorated and ready to receive guests on December 16. Spanish moss, flowers, and colored paper lanterns dress the house, and an altar with pine branches and moss is erected in one room. On the altar is a Nativity scene or *nacimiento,* which may be simple or elaborate, but which always includes a stable with figures of Mary and Joseph beside an empty cradle.

Many families may join in the *posada,* or the ceremony may be carried out at home by a single family. Nine families may combine to celebrate, meeting at a different house each night, which is a popular way to add to the social activity and entertaining.

The participants in the *posadas* are divided into two groups—the innkeepers and the pilgrims. The ceremony begins with the recitation of the Rosary. Each of the pilgrims is provided with a candle, and the procession, led by two children carrying images of Mary and Joseph, marches about the house. At the door of each room they sing, asking for shelter, and are refused until they come to the room where the altar has been set up. There the procession enters, with joyous songs, to pray before the altar and to place the figures of Mary and Joseph in the stable. The manger remains empty until the ninth night, which is Christmas Eve.

After the procession the religious part of the evening comes to an end. A party follows, with fireworks, food, and the excitement of the piñata. The piñata is an earthenware bowl covered in bright paper and gay with bright streamers. It is made in a great variety of sizes and shapes—a ship, an airplane, a donkey, a bird. The piñata is suspended above a doorway or from the ceiling, in the house or in the courtyard, and each child is given a turn at breaking it with a long stick. This is made difficult, as the piñata may be raised and lowered and the child is blindfolded. When at last the jar is broken, there is a merry scramble for the gifts and candy which pour out.

The last of the *posadas*, on Christmas Eve, is solemn and impressive. The child who leads the procession carries the Infant Jesus. When the pilgrims are admitted to the room which has the altar, everyone kneels, and the father of the house offers a prayer. While a special hymn is sung, the father takes the figure of the Holy Child and places it in the manger as all the candles around the altar are lighted.

The festivities of the piñata party follow, but are interrupted for attendance at midnight Mass. Christmas Day is quiet, but the house is filled with flowers and the dinner is prepared with great care. Roast turkey is served, with tortillas and fried peppers, and a dish of fruits and vegetables beautifully garnished. No gifts are exchanged on Christmas Day, but souvenirs are given to guests at Christmas dinner.

Mexican children receive their gifts on Epiphany. Before this day they write letters to the Christ Child, and on the Eve of Epiphany place their shoes on the window sill or balcony to await the visit of the Magi. The day is celebrated in the churches with beautiful music and thousands of lighted candles in an expression of joy at the birth of Jesus.

American influence has brought the Christmas tree to some parts of Mexico with the result that some children get gifts both on Christmas and Epiphany.

PIÑATAS (PLAIN)

MATERIALS:

paper cups with rolled rims and pointed bottoms
gold, silver, and colored paints
pipe cleaners

DIRECTIONS:

1. Two cups are used for each piñata. Insert the ends of a pipe cleaner through the pointed end of one cup. Spread the ends of pipe cleaner inside the cup and leave loop outside for hanger.
2. Place rims of two cups together and stitch with heavy-duty thread (use tapestry needle) around the rims.
3. Spray with gold, silver, or colored spray paint. When dry, paint small designs, using various kinds and colors of paint. Use your imagination in decorating the piñatas.

PIÑATAS (CREPE PAPER)

MATERIALS:

paper cups with rolled rims and pointed bottoms
crepe paper
pipe cleaners

DIRECTIONS:

1. Follow steps 1 and 2 for plain piñatas.
2. Cut strips of crepe paper 2" wide, using various colors of paper.
3. With sewing machine, gather through the

center of each strip, then ruffle the edges of paper.

4. Apply glue along the center of each strip and attach to the cups, either lengthwise or around the cups.

5. To the bottom of the piñata attach a shredded crepe-paper tail, 5″ or 6″ in length.

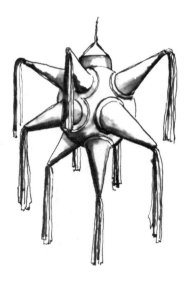

Note: Great imagination can be used in these piñatas. Decorate them with solid colors, mixed colors, stripes, ruffles, mixed colored tails, etc. There are many variations and sizes of piñatas. An excellent book, *Piñatas*, by Virginia Brock (see Resources), describes the many shapes and styles and the various methods of construction.

PAPER LANTERNS

MATERIALS:

Madras paper, 3 sheets to package
bright beads or inexpensive costume jewelry

DIRECTIONS:

1. For the small-sized lantern, cut the package of paper into three 8″ lengthwise strips. For the large size, cut package into two 12″ lengthwise strips.

2. Using any good paper glue, make paper into one long strip. Let seams dry completely.

3. Pleat paper into ¾″ pleats the entire length. Make a crease through the center, then unfold.

4. Join the last pleat to the first pleat to form a cylinder. Sew pleats together ½″ from top and bottom of cylinder. At the top leave enough thread to make a loop for hanging.

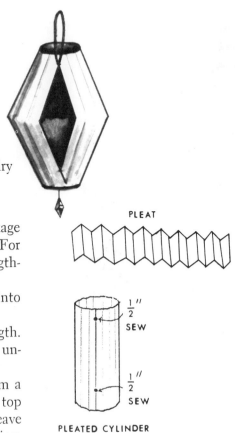

PLEAT

1″/2
SEW

1″/2
SEW

PLEATED CYLINDER

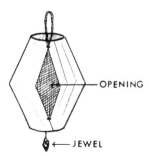

At the bottom fasten a bright bead or inexpensive jewel.

5. By working through the opening, puff out the pleating to form the lantern. Push the ends together to aid in puffing out the pleating.

ALUMINUM ORNAMENTS

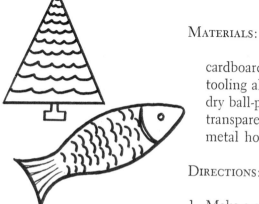

MATERIALS:

cardboard patterns
tooling aluminum
dry ball-point pen or round-tipped stylus
transparent paint
metal hooks

DIRECTIONS:

1. Make a cardboard pattern of fish, bird, Christmas tree, star, pineapple, or pear.
2. Trace pattern on tooling aluminum with pencil. Cut out with scissors.
3. With a DRY ball-point pen or stylus indent the details of the design (wings and eyes on the birds, scales on the fish, etc.).
4. Paint with a transparent paint which coats metal, glass, or plastic, such as Cryst-L-Craze.
5. Puncture a small hole at top and hang with metal hook.

POSADA

Pottery clay can be used to mold the figures of the Mexican Nativity scene. These include men, women, children, choir boys, and animals. Allow the clay figures to dry thoroughly before painting with tempera.

Add small items such as fabric head

162

scarves, miniature straw hats, baskets, flowers, and candles.

WHITE DOVES

White doves for a Mexican tree may be purchased.

STAINED
GLASS
TREE

The origin of stained glass is obscure, but it is not likely that the art goes further back than the ninth century. Actually the earliest reference to stained glass in the accepted sense of the term—windows colored, but pictorial also—is a manuscript which records that Adalbéron, Bishop of Rheims from 969 to 988, rebuilt the cathedral and redecorated it with windows representing various stories. There is a reference to earlier colored windows, but they were not pictorial. Evidence seems to favor certain windows in Augsburg Cathedral, with figures of the prophets, as the earliest windows extant, and these may date from the middle of the eleventh century.

It cannot be stated with certainty when and where glass was invented, but the oldest examples of glass work known have come from the Egyptian tombs. Glass products were shipped from Egypt to Greece and Rome, and soon Egypt was no longer the center of glassmaking. Rome became the main source, but glass was also made in Greece. Travelers to Rome spoke of the mosaic pictures made of glass in Greece. These mosaics were really the forerunner of the stained glass or colored glass window.

Mosaics were made many years before the birth of Christ, but it was the Christian church which brought about their widespread use. Mosaics were made by fitting small pieces of colored glass into damp plaster to make a picture or design, and mosaics of Christ, the Apostles, and Bible stories were used to decorate the interior of early Christian churches.

By the ninth and tenth centuries the organization of the church divided Christian churches into districts, each presided over by a bishop. The bishops took great pride in building beautiful churches in their districts and there was great rivalry to outdo each other in size and beauty of the cathedrals. The development of Gothic architecture, with its many windows, left little space for mosaics on the interior, so workmen adapted the mosaic idea to the windows and developed a decoration even richer than before.

Soon the artists learned that designs could be made in glass not only for beauty but for the purpose of instruction. The stained glass windows served as textbooks for those who could not read or those who had no books. Two of the earliest windows can be seen in the Augsburg Cathedral in Germany and in the Cathedral at Le Mans in France. King David and the prophets are in the picture in the Augsburg window, and the Ascension in the window at Le Mans.

The golden age of stained glass in France was the period of the twelfth and thirteenth centuries. At this time the artist and glass-blower worked on the grounds of the cathedral. The artist drew the design in full size on whitened boards that were used as his work-bench, and the first lines indicated the iron bars that were necessary to hold the window firmly, for a large sheet of glass and lead was too pliable to withstand the force of wind and weather. These bars played into the design and determined the main lines of the composition. Small pieces of glass, usually not more than an inch long, were cut from sheets of glass which had been colored while in the molten state by the addition of coloring matter.

The artist was always mindful of the harmony of the design when light penetrated the window, and did not hesitate—when the design called for it—to have the Prodigal Son feeding one green pig and two blue ones. The rich purple color did not always result from purple glass, but might be achieved by placing side by side small bits of red and blue, allowing the eye to mix them at a distance. This resulted in a richer hue than that of purple glass. Here and there in the design a larger piece of glass was used on which a face, hand, or bit of drapery was painted with a brownish enamel. The pieces were fired to fuse the enamel with the glass.

The story of Christmas has been told in many of the stained glass windows, such as the center window of the Cathedral of Notre Dame showing the Virgin Mary with the Infant Jesus on her knees. At Canterbury there are windows showing the Magi following the star, and again the Magi making their offerings to the Infant Christ.

In nineteenth-century America stained glass windows were designed for the Gothic churches which were being constructed. After much research craftsmen were able to produce windows technically as fine as those in Europe. All the styles that appeared in early churches and many new ones can be seen in the windows in America today. The Washington Cathedral has windows which copy the formula, methods, and thought of medieval windows. Another cathedral with great windows is St. John the Divine in New York City. Today's church architect uses stained glass for the modern church, replacing the story-telling window with one in which symbolism is expressed in bright color and design.

Present-day artists find stained glass an inspirational medium for decorative pieces designed for modern homes as well as public buildings.

Stained glass and liquid plastic resin provide the handicraftsman of today with materials for charming designs for hanging in windows or decorating Christmas trees. Small pieces of glass are fitted inside a band of lead or copper and held in place by the resin, which hardens overnight. These decorative pieces have the advantage of being light in weight, since lead is not used to hold the inside pieces together; they are easy to make and inexpensive.

STAINED GLASS ORNAMENTS

MATERIALS:

masking tape, 2", 3", or 4"—4" if available
lead stripping, ⅛" wide
stained glass, broken or cut in random sizes (round glass nuggets may also be used in many designs)
liquid plastic resin and its catalyst

DIRECTIONS:

1. Select a simple drawing 6" or smaller in size. Free-form or conventional patterns may also be used.
2. For easy handling roll the lead stripping into

a coil. Shape it along the contour lines of the pattern; at the end overlap pattern outline about ¾″ and cut. (Tweezers are helpful in shaping around curves and corners.) The lead stripping stands on its edge, does not lie flat; this makes a frame for the design.

3. Put strips of wide masking tape together to make a sheet larger than the design. Carefully lift the lead contour design to the sticky side of the masking tape and press down to secure to tape.

4. For inside pattern lines cut and shape lead and press into position on tape.

5. Fit stained glass pieces in selected colors appropriate for the design into lead pattern as in a jigsaw puzzle, filling in as solidly as possible. Make use of tiny slivers of glass between pieces, as cut edges of glass give sparkle to finished ornament.

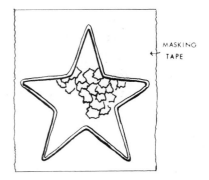

MASKING TAPE

6. Mix plastic resin and catalyst according to directions on can. Drip the plastic resin over the design; be sure there is resin in all small cracks. Any resin which flows from under the lead stripping may be removed with a toothpick after the resin becomes the consistency of gelatin.

7. Allow 6 to 8 hours for resin to harden.

8. Peel the masking tape from the ornament and place the ornament face down on a cellophane or plastic sheet to allow the bottom side, which is "tacky" from masking tape, to harden.

9. Drill a small hole into resin at desired point of balance, about ⅛″ from lead edge. The hole may be made with a sharp ice pick heated on stove unit. Any rough edges of hardened resin on lead may be removed by filing or by a heated knife. Be careful with heated knife and ice pick, as lead melts easily.

10. Hang ornament with monofilament (fishing) line. Use a double strand looped through the hole.

JAPAN

Christmas was unknown in Japan until a century ago. Today the Christian population celebrates the day with religious meaning, and it has also become a popular holiday for those who do not profess Christianity.

When the Christmas season approaches, there is great activity in the stores. In the cities one sees festive decorations, even Christmas trees with lights and ornaments and Santa Claus with reindeer. Shoppers throng the streets, creating a year-end business boom which has been actively encouraged by merchants. There is a great spirit of gaiety as more and more Japanese express interest in Christmas as a holiday season.

This is not surprising in a country where festivals have been a part of civilization for a thousand years. Some are religious festivals of a faithful people, some celebrate an event in history or honor an ancient scholar. Many are for children. The great love of the Japanese for children is manifested in such days as Girls' Day, Boys' Day, and Big Kite-flying Day. There is a ceremonial festival when children and parents visit shrines with pride and thankfulness for the health of children who have reached the ages of seven, five, and three.

Girls' Day, on the third day of the third month, evidences respect and closeness among family members. On Boys' Day, the fifth day of the fifth month, every home with a son has a tall pole in the garden or on the roof of the house to which is attached a great kite-like fish of paper or silk. The fish (carp) symbolizes fortitude, courage, and perseverance, and the wish of the day is that each boy in the family will have health, vigor, and success in his undertakings. These festivals are centuries old.

A relatively new holiday honors all children of the country, bringing attention to the importance of respecting the character of children and of children expressing their gratitude to parents.

The manufacture of Japanese goods for the Christmas markets of the world and an ever-increasing communication with other countries has combined with this love of children to popularize Christmas. Christmas trees are decorated with small toys and dolls, fluted paper ornaments, and candies in gay wrappings. Santa Claus is a kind old man who is supposed to have eyes in the back of his head to observe children's behavior.

New Year's Day is the most keenly enjoyed and widely celebrated event of the Japanese calendar. Many of the practices of this season resemble those of the Western world at Christmas. There is a thorough housecleaning, and traditional decorations of pine, bamboo, and apricot are used. The *kadomatsu* (gate pine) is set on either side of the front entrance; this is a decoration not seen at any other time of the year. Special food is eaten during the holiday, and friendship is the keynote of the season. Calls are made to homes of friends, relatives, and business acquaintances, and gifts of all kinds are given. Children make the most of the holiday, as the boys enjoy their kite-flying and girls engage in the sport of battledore and shuttlecock.

As in many other countries, the holiday is a time for seeing auguries of the future. In Japan, the second night of the New Year is a time for foretelling the future for those who believe in dreams. A ship laden with treasure naturally portends happy and prosperous days. To dream of an earthquake means a change of residence; a sea voyage or a rising sun foretells good fortune. A dream of rain means that worries may be expected.

There is a serious side to the holiday as seen in visits to shrines, the messages of joy and good will to others, and resolutions of high purpose in the New Year. Just as the Christmas season lasts several days or weeks in the Christian world, the New Year festivities in Japan continue with various events until January 20.

BIRD TREE

A custom of northern European countries which gives great charm to Christmas is the special attention to animals and birds. This act is one of veneration for the creatures who were present at the birth of Christ.

In Sweden, Christmas Eve was the morning when the sheaf for birds was put out. The tradition is still observed, but a bit differently from olden days when each household tried to set its sheaf a little higher than the neighbor's. The ancient belief was that the family which could set its sheaf the highest would be the luckiest during the coming year, so farm families raised the sheaves on long poles high in the air. Later no competition was involved, and the sheaf went up outside the window where the pleasure of watching the birds could be enjoyed.

In Norway the best sheaves selected at threshing time were put on poles in the yard and on top of the barn. After preparations were finished on Christmas Eve, the head of the household would go out to see if there were many sparrows on the Christmas sheaf. If there were many, a good corn year was indicated. If a sparrow lighted before the work of putting up the sheaf was finished, it foretold death in the family.

In Denmark all nature is glorified at the Christmas season. For the birds bits of suet and bread are hung on trees, and the best sheaves of the harvest are put out in many locations around the farm and home grounds. When the birds come to eat in great numbers, a year of good crops is foretold. The farm animals receive extra portions of food with the wish, "Eat well, this is Christmas Eve."

In Poland sheaves of wheat are used to decorate the house and are later scattered in the orchards for the birds. In some parts of Hungary it was the custom to reserve the sheaf for a bird feast on New Year's Day, and in south Germany corn was strewn on the housetops.

The custom of caring for the birds is still observed in Scandinavian countries, and is one of the cherished links with the past for these people who value so highly their old traditions. Even in the cities the sheaf of oats or wheat hangs on apartment balcony or terrace for the wintering birds. Boxes of suet and seed invite the birds to join the Christmas feast. In the United States bird sheaves may be seen in Minnesota, Wisconsin, Illinois, and North Dakota, where the Scandinavians have brought an Old World custom to a new home.

Many Americans, prompted by kindness, love of nature, and an interest in conservation, provide feeding stations and a planting of natural foods for birds throughout the year. Perhaps a discarded Christmas tree with remnants of cranberry and popcorn strings inspired the idea of a special treat at Christmas time. A discarded tree provides shelter as well; many trees, such as the balsam, hold needles well into the spring, sheltering the birds during the coldest months of the year. The flash of the cardinal's wings brings happiness to the American bird-watcher just as the sight of the red-vested *Domherrar* charms the Swedish householder who sets up the traditional sheaf of grain.

BIRD FEEDER

MATERIALS:

    4" aluminum foil pan
    ½" mesh hardware cloth, 8½" x 4"
    red paint
    red pipe cleaner
    12" piece of red ribbon

DIRECTIONS:

1. Make a cylinder of the hardware cloth. Place cylinder in foil pan and push ends of wire through to bottom. Bend wires to hold basket in place.

BEND THESE WIRES

2. Paint feeder bright red. Run a red ribbon around the hardware cloth at center. Attach red pipe cleaner for handle.
3. Fill the basket with 1″ squares of suet and place grain in pan.

POPCORN STRINGS

With heavy-duty thread or twine, string popcorn in 24″ lengths and hang vertically in 12″ loops. Wire to tree.

MARSHMALLOW STICK

String six marshmallows on small-sized wire. Tie a bow of red ribbon at bottom and hang vertically on tree.

DOUGHNUTS

Decorate doughnut with a sprig of red-berried holly. Loop a red ribbon through hole in doughnut; hang to tree by wire.

CRANBERRY RINGS

String cranberries on wire strong enough to hold its shape when drawn into a circle. Tie cranberries into a 4″ circle, leaving enough wire for hanging.

ORANGE BASKET

Make three holes equidistant around the edge of half an orange shell. Push ends of a 12″ pipe cleaner through two of the holes; push the end of another pipe cleaner through third hole and twist it around the center of first pipe cleaner. Leave the remaining 6″ for hanger. Fill with nut meats and cranberries.

PINE CONES

Twist florist wire around pine cone and fasten, leaving a length for hanging. Spread peanut butter on crevices of pine cones and wire to tree.

TREETOP ORNAMENT

MATERIALS:

6″ styrofoam ball
stalks of millet and sorghum
green gumdrops, leaf-shaped
peanuts in shell
heavy wire or pieces of coat hanger
3′ dowel, ½″ size
small florist's picks

DIRECTIONS:

1. Mount the styrofoam on the 3′ dowel, reinforcing around dowel with glue.
2. Push wire through peanut shells, using 8 to 12 peanuts. Use as many wires as desired; they may also vary in length. Glue around the wire where it goes into the ball, so that it will remain steady and secure.
3. Force stalks of millet and sorghum into styrofoam ball.
4. Cover surface of ball with green gumdrops. These can be held in place with florist's picks.
5. Wire the dowel to the leader of the tree so that the ornament centers the treetop.

RESOURCES

BOOKS

Christmas. An annual publication from Augsburg Press, Minneapolis.

The Christmas Book, by Francis X. Weiser. New York: Harcourt, Brace, 1952.

Christmas Customs Around the World, by Herbert H. Wernecke. Philadelphia: Westminster Press, 1959.

Christmas and Its Customs, by Christina Hole. New York: M. Barrows and Company, 1958.

Christmas Everywhere, by Elizabeth Hough Sechrist. Revised edition. Philadelphia: Macrae-Smith, 1962.

Christmas Helps, 1966. New York: Family Circle, Inc.

The Christmas Tree, by Daniel J. Foley. Philadelphia: Chilton Books, 1960.

Christmas the World Over, by Daniel J. Foley. Philadelphia: Chilton Books, 1963.

Customs and Holidays Around the World, by Lavinia Dobler. New York: Fleet Publishing Corp., 1962.

A New Look at Christmas Decorations, by Sister Gratia Listaite and Norbert A. Hildebrand. Milwaukee: Bruce Publishing Company, 1957.

Once upon a Christmas Time, by Thyra Ferré Bjorn. New York: Holt, Rinehart & Winston, 1964.

The Pageantry of Christmas. The Life Book of Christmas, Vol. II. New York: Time, Inc.

Piñatas, by Virginia Brock. Nashville: Abingdon Press, 1966.

Singing Windows, by Mary Young. Nashville: Abingdon Press, 1962.

The Southern Christmas Book, by Harnett T. Kane. New York: McKay, 1958.

Swedish Christmas Celebrations. Gothenburg, Sweden: Tre Tryckare, 1963.
(Four books in one: "Swedish Christmas Food," by John Sjöstrand; "Recipes for Swedish Christmas Food," by John Sjöstrand and Brigit Björck; "Christmas Decorations," by Goran Axel-Nilsson; "Christmas Songs and Games," by Gösta Lundborg.)

American Handicrafts Company
   1011 Foch Street, Fort Worth, Texas   76101
      A good source of many types of handicraft materials. Write to this
      address for the location of the store nearest you.
The Gift Shop
   Reception Center, 614 South Main Street, Winston-Salem, North Caro-
   lina   27101
      Carries Moravian stars, beeswax candles.
Gifts from the Heart
   Box 1197, Scotia, New York   12302
      Can supply the cutouts for the Danish tree.
Lee Wards
   840 North State, Elgin, Illinois   60120
      Another source of handicraft materials.
Liturgical Press
   Collegeville, Minnesota   56321
      Can supply patterns for the Jesse Tree symbols.
The Moravian Book Shop
   428 Main Street, Bethlehem, Pennsylvania   18018
      Moravian stars and beeswax candles.
Paprikas Weiss, Importer
   1546 Second Avenue, New York, New York   10028
      Various types of candles and candle holders.
Shopping International, Inc.
   850 Shopping International Building, Norwich, Vermont   05055
      Carries the snowballs for the Swedish tree.

INDEX

C

D

E

L

M

N

O

P